Praise for A Living Label

This book is personal, it is inspirational, and it is practical. All of us will benefit from reading it, as Bukola shares both personal and professional experiences. Her goal is always the same-to provide hope and encouragement so that survivors will be empowered.

- **Florrie Burke, Human Rights and anti-trafficking consultant.**

Bukola's contribution to the Advisory Council, and this book, reflect her incredible depth of understanding of, and empathy for, the struggle that trafficking survivors face long after they have escaped their trafficking situation and received the most basic of services to help them recover.

- **Melysa Sperber, director of the Alliance to End Slavery and Trafficking (ATEST)**

I am grateful for the privilege given to me to write in ALL book. I pray it touches the heart of everybody that reads it, and that it helps survivors as well.

- **Anuoluwapo Ogunmola, Owner, House of Fancy**

Here we are "The Living label" - a living testimony. Thank you for taking such a pain to write this to help others. You are like a mirror and a light for others to see and know that there is hope in every situation.

- **Abolaji Ogunmola**

As a very committed advocate, Bukola adamantly uses her journalist skills and tech skills to create educational material for publications, for T. V. and websites, for civic groups, and for school textbooks.

- **Annette Brandner**

A Living Label is an opportunity to understand the complex nature of Bukola's journey, and I look forward to continuing to learn every lesson I can through these pages.

- **Sarah Leistico, Social Justice Organizer & SAASI U.S. Coordinator, Based in Minneapolis- St. Paul, MN**

I am not surprised that she could turn her story around from an imprisoned soul to a living label after climbing so many ladders to be where she is today.

- **Rose EJEMBI is a Senior Correspondent with The Sun Newspapers (Nigeria).**

Trafficking is a terrible, terrible, thing. It destroys people's lives, their souls, and the people around it suffer as well. It is evil through and through and it can be happening right in front of us, hidden in plain sight.

- **Joe Hesch – "Uncle Joe"**

Anyone can become a victim of human trafficking. Bukola was a journalist in Nigeria and a woman of incredible strength and intelligence. If she can become a victim of human trafficking, anyone can. The situation, not the characteristics of the individual, is the primary factor in this crime.

- **Dr. Sherry Jordon, Associate Professor, University of St. Thomas, St. Paul, MN**

I wish you all the best in your new book "A Living Label" and in your future. Thank you for taking your time to write this book and for designing the money resulting of the sales to help survivors in need.

- **Ronny Marty, Member, U.S. Advisory Council on Human Trafficking**

Bukola's story is a gift to all, especially to African women and girls because they can easily relate to her experiences and understand the context.

- **Rita Apaloo**

Bukola is a survivor. She is resilient and tenacious. When she was able, she turned her altruistic deeds outward to help other abuse and human trafficking victims.

- **Elyse Kaner is a retired reporter and arts editor for ABC Newspapers in Minnesota.**

I was so moved by your courage and tenacity that I wanted to become a part of whatever you were doing for the cause of trafficking.

Yvette R. Toko, Owner, Healing Words with Yvette

Bukola's story made me think and look at life from different angles.

Isabella Kerubo Ongera, Vinbel Foundation

Students gained disciplinary and civic benefits while design problem solving for the mobile TV set for the Imprisoned Show dedicated to advocating for victims of human trafficking on Minnesota public television with show producer, Bukola Oriola.

Dr. Abimbola O. Asojo, University of Minnesota

OTHER TITLES BY BUKOLA ORIOLA

Imprisoned: The Travails of a Trafficked Victim

The Natural Hair Softness Headaches: 6 items in your kitchen or drug store you will find helpful

Quit Your Day Job!: Five steps to turn your passion to money using blogging and social media

Simple Steps to Hair Braiding

A Living Label

AN INSPIRATIONAL MEMOIR AND GUIDE

Bukola Oriola

A Living Label

Printed in the United States © 2016, by Bukola Oriola

ISBN: 978-0-9981817-4-5 (Paperback)

October 2016 Bukola Oriola (Bukola Braiding & Beauty Supply, LLC) 1628 County Highway 10 Suite 210 Spring Lake Park MN 55432

Phone: 763-433-9454.

Websites: www.bukolabraiding.com, www.bukolaoriola.com

Emails: info@bukolabraiding.com, info@bukolaoriola.com

Editors: Ann Brown, Ann Brown Communications, Washington, D.C., Dr. Nora Flom, Blaine, Minnesota, and Shereen Rubenstein, Chevy Chase, Maryland.

Foreword by Florrie Burke, Human Rights and anti-trafficking consultant.

Cover image: Chris Dang Photography

Cover Outfit designed by House of Fancy

Dedication

I dedicate this book, "A Living Label" to my son, Samuel, who endured the agony of human trafficking and domestic violence with me, became a survivor, and is now advocating with me.

Table of Contents

Acknowledgement

I will like to thank God Almighty for giving me a second chance to live and to advocate for other survivors of human trafficking and domestic violence. I am also very grateful for all the people that He has brought my way to get me to where I am today. I have a long list of people to thank but I would like to ask to be pardoned for those whose names have not been highlighted on the list.

I would like to thank my editors, Ann Brown of Ann Brown Communications, Washington D.C., Dr. Nora Flom, Minnesota, and Shereen Rubenstein, Chevy Chase, Maryland for helping me present my thoughts in a clear and concise manner. I am very grateful to all those who have written pieces for this book: Anuoluwapo Ogunmola, Abolaji Ogunmola, Sarah Leistico, Joe Hesch, Florrie Burke, Melysa Sperber, Roseline Ejembi, Rita Apaloo, Honorable Ronny Marty, Annette Brandner, Dr. Sherry Jordon, Elyse Kaner, Dr. Abimbola Asojo, and Isabella Kerubo Ongera.

I am full of gratitude to my siblings, friends, extended family, my church community at Anoka United Methodist Church, present and past board members of The Enitan Story, my instructors at Anoka Ramsey Community College and Metropolitan State University, the Student Senate at both higher

1

education institutions, Lulu Publishing CEC, Nigel Lee and his staff, the U.S. Consulate Public Affairs Section, Lagos, Nigeria, the director and staff at the National Agency for the Prohibition of Trafficking in Persons (NAPTIP), the staff and students of the Bells University, Ota, Federal University of Agriculture, Abeokuta, Lagos State Polytechnic, Ikorodu, University of Lagos, Yaba College of Technology, Rotary Club of Akute, District 9110, the U.S. Department of State Office to Monitor and Combat Trafficking in Persons, the offices of Congressman Keith Ellison and Senator Al Franken, Bukola Braiding clients, fellow survivors, and everyone who has been supportive throughout my journey from victim to survivor, and now advocate.

And, of course, my son, Samuel, who survived and is now advocating with me.

Foreword

H OW EXCITING and gratifying it is for me to write about Bukola Oriola and her new book, "A Living Label." This book continues to chronicle her journey as a survivor/advocate, but it is much more than that-it is a lesson in motivation, perseverance and faith. Human trafficking is a crime with perpetrators exploiting their victims in a variety of ways that result in financial gain for the traffickers and loss of dignity and personal agency for the victims. "A Living Label" illuminates possibilities and opportunities for survivors of this crime to move forward and to be the people they want to be. The exciting contribution of this book is how Bukola Oriola expands the meaning of survivor. She is more than her story: she has moved to a place where she can not only assist others on their journey, but she is able to transfer information, guidance and experience to those in her home country and beyond.

As someone who has worked in the field of human trafficking and worker exploitation for twenty years, I have long recognized the need for survivor representation that is genuine, respected and valued. Survivors are the experts because they have lived the experience of trafficking. Their experiences have always informed my work and that of my colleagues in the Freedom Network. At this point in the movement, there are survivors like Bukola who are partners in our work. They help service providers develop best practices, they work with law enforcement to educate them about the complexities of the crime, and they advocate with policy and lawmakers to improve the responses to this problem.

President Obama also recognized the importance of the survivor voice and created the first U.S. Advisory Council on Human Trafficking. Bukola Oriola is on this council and her book reflects the challenges and successes of survivor leadership. In 2013, I was honored to receive the first Presidential Award for outstanding efforts in combating human trafficking. In his presentation, Secretary of State John Kerry acknowledged my contribution to and insistence on a survivor centered approach grounded in human rights. I am proud of the advances in the field, but well aware that we still fall short of full inclusiveness and partnerships between survivors and those professionals doing the work. There are current gaps in education, experience, skill building and leadership development that prevent full representation of survivors in this work. It is important that we look at parts of this book as the guide it is meant to be and find the resources that can reduce these gaps and promote a seat at every table for survivor input and leadership.

Post-trafficking social and legal services are important, but as "A Living Label" points out, economic opportunities for survivors are scarce. To enhance stability and sustainability, survivor contributions must be recognized and compensated. Treat these

4

important survivor voices as the experts and compensate their inclusion as you would the professionals in the field. We must now focus on skill building and economic development so that survivors can reach the potential they have and live the life they might now only imagine.

This book is personal, it is inspirational, and it is practical. All of us will benefit from reading it, as Bukola shares both personal and professional experiences. Her goal is always the same-to provide hope and encouragement so that survivors will be empowered. I have studied trauma for forty years and have worked with hundreds of survivors. It is truly generous that in her book Bukola shares the highlights as well as her low points. I reread the following sentence multiple times as it moved me deeply, "It felt as if the sun stopped and the whole earth stood still." Bukola's story is hers, but she shares openly the steps she has taken along the way to becoming a strong advocate. She gives practical strategies to others, both to survivors and to professionals in the field. Bukola Oriola was able to write this book because she has used her curiosity, her diligence, her work ethic, and her sensibilities to assist others. This book reflects a culture of storytelling and Bukola created her organization, The Enitan Story, using the Yoruba word for 'someone telling a story.'

I am happy to know Bukola and to have played a very small part in this remarkable journey of hers. One message among many that I got from this book is, "Don't Label-Empower!"

Florrie Burke, Human Rights and anti-trafficking consultant.

Picture by Chris Dang Photography

"Survivors fill a unique gap in the fight against human trafficking."

- Bukola Oriola

Introduction

THIS BOOK, "A Living Label," is a memoir and a guide. In it, I chronicle my journey as a survivor, advocate, and subject matter expert to advocate for victims who are still enduring the agonies of human trafficking and domestic violence. Additionally, I hope that this book will provide inspiration to other survivors and practical solutions to nonprofit organizations, government agencies, and the general public on how to engage survivors in a way that is not re-exploitative, but mutually beneficial to the survivors and whoever is engaging the survivors as subject matter experts. I also document some of the daring ventures that I embarked upon as an advocate, such as a trip to Nigeria called Bringing the Story Back Home to educate my community and hopefully enlighten the youths about the dangers of "greener pastures" which might be a potential trap to becoming a victim of human trafficking.

In this book I do not talk about my story as a victim. For that story, kindly refer to my first memoir, "Imprisoned: The Travails of a Trafficked Victim." I documented my experience as a victim of human trafficking and domestic violence seven years ago to let other victims know that help is available and that they can overcome their own oppression. "Imprisoned: The Travails of a Trafficked Victim" explained one of the ways that a person can become a victim of human trafficking. It demonstrated that human trafficking is a multifaceted crime and can happen to anybody regardless of their status, educational background, career, family, culture, race, age, or gender. It revealed that human trafficking can be committed by a family member, it can include the additional crimes of domestic violence or sexual assault, and it can involve types of trafficking beyond the scope of sex trafficking, the type most discussed in the media.

I didn't hold back in my first memoir. I divulged in how I became a victim of human trafficking. My ex-husband exploited me for labor. I suffered isolation, hunger, and trauma in the form of physical, psychological, and emotional abuse, at the hands of the man who was supposed to be my protector. I almost lost my life in the process. In fact, I attempted suicide but I was lucky to survive because of my son, Samuel, whom you will read about in the following chapters. I often am questioned about Samuel by those who read my first book. Readers want to know what happened to him, where he is now, or how he is doing. I wrote about his well-being in this book. Finally, I have included writing pieces from my family, friends and associates about myself, my son, my work, and the connections they have with me on my journey thus far.

Although I had an associate degree in mass communication from my home country of Nigeria and practiced journalism for six years prior to becoming a victim of human trafficking in the United

States, my career and educational goals took a different turn as a survivor. I will share some of the steps that I took, such as returning to school, and how my parents ingrained the importance of education in me since childhood. You will also learn about some of my achievements as an advocate. I hope that survivors can understand and own the value of their stories without feeling timid or guilty asking for compensation. Equally importantly, I hope the public and allies will understand that survivors' stories provide essential knowledge and information that undoubtedly deserve compensation.

For informational purposes, the Trafficking Victims Protection Act of 2000 (TVPA) defines "severe forms of trafficking in persons" as follows:

> Sex trafficking: the recruitment, harboring, transportation, provision, or obtaining of a person for the purpose of a commercial sex act, in which the commercial sex act is induced by force, fraud, or coercion, or in which the person induced to perform such act has not attained 18 years of age.

> In the TVPA, the term "commercial sex act" means any sex act on account of which anything of value is given to or received by any person. (HHS, 2012).

> Labor Trafficking: the recruitment, harboring, transportation, provision, or obtaining of a person for

9

labor or services, through the use of force, fraud, or coercion for the purpose of subjection to involuntary servitude, peonage, debt bondage, or slavery.

I have provided this definition for those who might be learning about human trafficking for the first time or for those who do not fully understand all that it may include. Clearly, human trafficking is a criminal act that goes beyond solely sex trafficking.

In summary, I will share with readers my life's purpose, my challenges, my accomplishments and why I am happy to have a second chance to live – my life from victim to becoming the current secretary of the U.S. Advisory Council on Human Trafficking.

Be inspired!

Bukola Oriola takes a selfie with the Secretary of State, John Kerry at the White House in January 2016 during the inauguration of the U.S. Advisory Council on Human Trafficking.

Bukola Oriola taking a selfie with the Secretary of State, John Kerry at the PITF meeting at the White House on October 24, 2016 after some members of the Council presented the First Annual Report of the U.S. Advisory Council on Human Trafficking.

Picture credit – Department of State Trafficking in Persons Office

Chapter 1

Putting My Face to My Story

THE FIRST time that I publicly shared the story of my experience as a victim of domestic violence and human trafficking was at Winona State University in February, 2009. I had been invited to speak alongside a pro bono immigration lawyer. After a long drive to St. Paul, Minnesota, I met with the lawyer and we headed to the university. It was a long and scenic two hour drive along the Mississippi River. On the right side of the snakelike road, houses sat high up on the hill as if they were in the sky. To our left, flowed the Mississippi River. When we arrived at the university, we were greeted by the organizer of the event who appeared very excited to see us. The lawyer introduced me to him as the "second" speaker and he led us to the room where the event was taking place. I was presenting my speech on this day to two different audiences.

Feeling very nervous, I held tightly onto my written speech and listened to the first speaker educate the audience about human trafficking and the role of the law. At the end of her presentation, it was my turn. I stood in front of the room. I began to read straight from my speech and then decided to switch and just speak from my heart. It was an emotional speech. I felt like I had just opened my heart to the audience and cried out and urged those who needed help to ask for it. The crowd was moved; I saw a few of them crying and wiping their faces. I realized that I had opened their eyes to see that human trafficking can and does occur right there in their own community. At the end of my presentation, I was surprised and elated to see the audience giving me a standing ovation.

Once the room settled back down, I took questions from the audience and was asked by an African immigrant, "What are you doing to take your story back to your home country?" My response was that I would go back to my country with my story, but I didn't know at the time that it would take me seven years to fulfill that promise. Receiving support from both the U.S. and Nigeria governments, I was able to take that trip and reach over 20 million people in one week! The U.S. Consulate in Nigeria made it possible through its network of local and international media. I feel grateful to all those who helped me to take my story back home. You will read further details about this trip later in this book, as it is one of my record breaking achievements as a victim turned advocate.

The evening's presentation was equally moving for both myself and the audience. As I drove away that night and headed back to my son, Samuel, I felt victorious that I had triumphed over my ordeal by being able to step out in public to share such a sad story. The supportive response from the audience raised my self-esteem and gave me confidence to be the voice for those who are too ashamed to speak out publicly. In addition, I felt relieved that I have now honored the deal I made with God when I was a victim desperately fighting for my life: If He allowed me to survive, I would bear the shame for others by going public with my story.

That day that began in St. Paul, Minnesota fully launched my public speaking career. I was invited to speak to both small and large groups, at churches, community events, conferences, media appearances, and at numerous other venues. It was during one such presentation, at the National Association of Social Workers Annual Conference in Bloomington, Minnesota, that one of the audience members asked if I had written a book and my response was, "No." She approached me afterwards to say, "You should write a book." One year later, my first book, "Imprisoned: The Travails of a Trafficked Victim," was published.

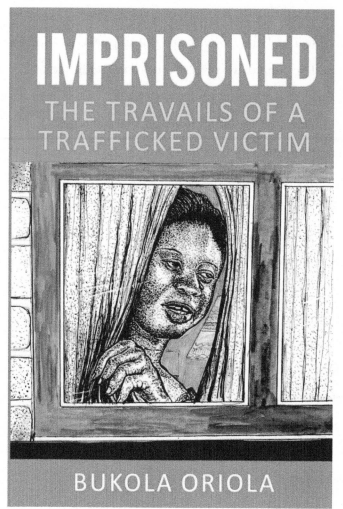

Imprisoned: The Travails of a Trafficked Victim book cover

Chapter 2

Going Back to School

I MUST profess that education is one of the main vehicles that has helped me transform from victim to survivor and now to advocate. I owe this to both of my late parents, as they impressed upon me the importance of education. My mother had the least education in the family, having not progressed past the elementary school level. Unfortunately, during her younger days, the culture believed in educating only the son in the family since he was the heir. Whenever my mother told me her painful story of being denied the right to go further in her academic studies, she reiterated her mission to make sure that her children got the education that she was denied. She sold her prized possessions to pay for our schooling. I witnessed my mother selling her gold jewelry at very low prices to gold dealers to support my father and to help pay school fees, books, specialized exams, uniforms, shoes, and all the numerous incidentals a child in school requires.

My father, unfortunately, was not able to continue his education beyond high school. Although he was a very brilliant man, his education was cut short because his mother's small trade, selling cooked rice and beans, couldn't support a college tuition. Furthermore, my grandfather did not see much value in education so he never paid for it. After high school, my father engaged in distance learning education and read many books. I grew up reading all kinds of books that I found on his bookshelf including science, fiction, and non-fiction books. He understood the value of education and was dedicated to paying for it himself despite the fact that he had very little money.

My mother was a trader, selling all kinds of items from groceries to kerosene, and for many years my father worked full time for several private Nigerian companies before starting his own business as an electrical contractor. I saw him fix TVs, radios, electrical problems in our house and neighbors' houses. Whenever he got a job to wire a newly built house, he hired one or two of his former colleagues to share the task and profit. He had all different kinds of gadgets sitting around the house and my brothers and I loved fiddling with all of them. I even learned how to use a tester as a young girl. In fact, my brothers and I thought that it was fun to check if there was current in a socket or not. Bright light shone in the tester's yellow plastic if the socket had electric current running through it and we were so fascinated by this that we played around with it more often than naught. Looking back now, I realize that I had inherited my entrepreneurial spirit from both of my

18

parents. They definitely taught me the importance of taking words and putting them into action.

When I was in high school, I loved working on various experiments whether they succeeded or failed. Sometimes I tried to mimic my father's electrical experiments but they didn't seem to work for me quite the way they did for him. However, I was very proud of an experiment that did work out fabulously for me. I built my own cooking stove using powdered and evaporated milk cans of various sizes. I attended a boarding school where we occasionally brought in uncooked food, which was regarded as contraband. We snuck it in and when we didn't have electricity to cook due to power outage, my stove proudly provided us with delicious cooked rice, soup, and beans.

After completing high school, I studied Mass Communications at The Polytechnic in Ibadan, Oyo State, Nigeria, and practiced journalism for six years. Having earned an associate degree I was eager to acquire a bachelor's degree as well. I began this additional education shortly before traveling to the United States for an assignment that was only supposed to last for a few weeks, but led me into two years of bondage as a victim of human trafficking and domestic violence.

I decided to return to school in Minnesota in 2012, but not solely for my bachelor's degree. It was because I had a mission – to obtain the academic certificate to advocate for victims and survivors of human trafficking, and to be paid for my services as a professional. I was quick to realize that people were interested in my story, and referred to me as the one "making the show." However, I was paid little or absolutely nothing. I was a single mother who had bills to pay just like every other working person. It was despairing to hear that the event organizer was paying a co-presenter with a Ph.D. $1,200 but was not willing to pay me for my time, despite the fact that I would be driving two hours one way to give my presentation. This is just one of many obstacles that I had to overcome as a survivor. I have had to turn down presentation opportunities where people or organizations thought that my story was important and needed to be told but offered no compensation for my time and expertise, even though funds were readily available.

Though I had been giving presentations for three years by 2012, one of the first classes I enrolled in when I returned to school was public speaking. I wanted to learn how to be more professional in my speaking engagements. I am thankful for that class. It was not only educational but also empowering for me. I learned how to tell my story in a constructive and professional manner, presenting my story as an example rather than revealing the entire story from beginning to the end, which usually left me emotionally drained. People noticed and even commented on my growth as a public speaker. Some had been around long enough to see me grow from looking as fragile as a newly laid egg, to triumphant and solid like a boiled egg. I am grateful to all those individuals, who not only follow my progress but also show their support through encouraging words, by volunteering for my projects, or donating to The Enitan Story. This is a nonprofit organization that I founded in 2013 to advocate for victims and empower survivors of human trafficking and domestic violence.

You can read some of my classroom essays at the end of this book.

Bukola Oriola's parents, Adesola and Sikiru Ogunmola

Chapter 3
Trial to Testimony

PEOPLE SAY to me over and over again, "You are courageous," "You are brave," or "You are a powerful woman." However, I see myself as a woman full of grace. I don't know how I would be where I am today without the potent grace of God upon my life. As a survivor, I am up against so many obstacles. I am a label, minimalized knowingly or unknowingly by close friends, associates, and worst of all, advocacy professionals, groups, or organizations. I constantly struggle to find my voice and to be heard. I am surprised and disheartened by the behavior of some individuals involved in advocacy organizations. It makes me wonder whether they are actually passionate about the cause and helping victims and survivors, or are solely focused on making money. I hear comments such as, "Human trafficking is where the money is now, because people will donate when you say that you are working with human trafficking victims." Interestingly, many organizations working on human trafficking issues seem to have sprung up overnight.

My message is simple and to the point: "Help is available." Indeed, I thought that death was the only way out when I was going through my ordeal as a victim of human trafficking and domestic violence. The process of getting help was very uncomfortable and very complicated. I had to stay hopeful while going through a system and culture that was unfamiliar. I cried. I prayed. I listened to music. A piece of a song that I listened to several times during my recovery at the battered women's shelter was by Smith Wigglesworth titled, "God Have Mercy." I cried to God for help to the point where I made a covenant with Him. As I shared earlier, I promised that I would put my face to my story and take the shame for those victims who couldn't show their face publicly due to the ordeal that they had experienced. When I finally received the help I so desperately needed, especially regarding my immigration status, I couldn't have been more grateful and willing to fulfill my side of the deal. The public speaking engagements and my first published book launched me into fulfilling my promise. I am grateful today that many women, men, and their children have received help because of my story.

From my own experience, I have learned that victims too often do not speak up or reach out for help because they don't believe that genuine support is available, especially in a foreign country where they don't know anybody. I have also come to understand that culture plays a very strong role in keeping a victim trapped in an abusive situation, especially in cultures where people are stigmatized and encouraged to stay silent about such issues. Some perpetrators constantly threaten foreign victims with deportation or humiliation in their primary communities. When a victim finally reaches out for help, their home community often turns against them rather than providing help. It is a battle that I still contend with today in my community. I have endured so many throat slashing comments and accusations from some of my community members. Even at the point when I needed help the most, some people who could have supported me turned away.

This is why I pleaded to God for help, and He has never failed. Has it been easy? The answer is, "No." However, trusting the invincible power of God has helped me to take little steps to move forward, at times surprising myself and my supporters. One powerful example of when I felt the presence of God was when I traveled to Nigeria for the Bringing the Story Back Home Tour. I initially planned the trip with zero dollars, except for the few minimal donations I received. Yet God showed up through the Metropolitan State University and the U.S. Consulate in Lagos, helping me to accomplish a tour that took place at five higher institutions in Nigeria and reached millions of people within and outside of my country. I executed a project whose budget exceeded $100,000, with less than $10,000 in cash. I don't know how I could have pulled that off without the presence of God and His potent power at work.

As a result of my own experience, I can say to you, "Relax and trust God. You don't need to know how, just believe Him and He will show up on your behalf and make you shine in the face of your adversaries."

Top: At North Metro TV, Blaine on Imprisoned Show set with Commander Brian Podany, Bottom - Left: The Enitan Story intern, Nora Kane in the control room, Middle: Anoka County Attorney, Attorney Tony Palumbo and Anoka County Sheriff, Sheriff James Stuart

Imprisoned Show was documented as one of the accomplishments of the Obama administration in the fight against human trafficking in 2014 when it hosted the Hubert Humphrey's fellows from Nepal, Vietnam, and Malaysia.

Chapter 4
Bringing the Story Back Home

HUMAN TRAFFICKING prevention is paramount in my mind. I believe that education is one of the most effective tools for preventing human trafficking or any form of abuse in the community. As mentioned earlier, my tour to Nigeria was a daring adventure. I had been trying to embark on the project for three years before I finally nailed it down. I had no money in the bank or in my wallet; I had no big funder or grantor, yet I was determined to educate Nigerian youth about the danger of human trafficking, using my own personal experience. I had reached out to several people in Nigeria and connected with old contacts and former colleagues. Some were supportive while others teased me with embarrassing comments posted on social media. I attempted to work with various people but when their intentions were unclear, I had to back out. I made phone calls and sent emails to numerous corporate organizations, both in the U.S. and in Nigeria, and got no reply. I spent hours writing and sending proposals that were never acknowledged, or I received only vague responses. For several months, I got little to no sleep trying to find help and support for this project. I must confess that listening to almost every one of Jesse Duplantis's videos on YouTube and the audio of the Power of Positive Thinking by Norman Vincent Peale, and other videos featuring Peale, helped me to build my faith and find a way to fulfill my personal mission.

I had rekindled my academic studies in Minnesota at Anoka Ramsey Community College in 2012 and transferred to a four-year institution, Metropolitan State University, in 2014. I enrolled in the individualized studies degree program with a focus on community leadership and diversity. I felt so grateful to be enrolled in this program because it allowed me to focus my academic work directly in line with my profession – human trafficking and domestic violence advocacy. From the first class that I sat in, I knew that I was in the right place. With the help of faculty who guided students with their student directed learning projects, I was able to design two independent study curriculums for my project, "Bringing the Story Back Home."

The first goal of my proposal was to engage students in human trafficking prevention through awareness, at five higher institutions in Nigeria. Secondly, I planned to speak with the media and educate them about the various ways in which someone could become a victim of human trafficking, ways not usually portrayed in the media. Additionally, I wanted to examine human trafficking as a typology of violence and evaluate the outcome of the responses of my audiences, and get the Nigerian youth involved. By applying the 'Spectrum of Prevention" my hope was to fully engage the students in the prevention of this typology of violence.

My first goal began to take shape during a summer semester human rights class at the university. This was partly due to the support I received from Florrie Burke, a rare gem and advocate in the anti-trafficking movement. I met Florrie when I was invited to speak on two panels at the Freedom Network Conference in Washington, D.C. in 2015. Aside from helping me with the draft proposal of my independent studies, she also agreed to have her name included as a reference on my independent studies proposal. She affects me as someone who is not just involved in the anti-trafficking movement, but one who genuinely cares and works to foster survivors' empowerment and leadership abilities. She gained my trust as a survivor because of her actions and not just her words. She continuously follows my progress and is always encouraging.

One of the most critical goals of my human trafficking awareness project was actually getting on a plane and arriving in Nigeria. An independent evaluator from the Minnesota Department of Health and Safety was hired to assist me in completing my independent studies. This was largely due to the fact that the study of human trafficking was relatively new in the academic arena, and no faculty member at the time was qualified to be my evaluator. I remember being asked in our first meeting whether I was going to implement my project by actually traveling or was I just traveling in theory. I told her that I absolutely intended

29

to take a trip to Nigeria. She was surprised and asked if I had the funding to make it happen. I told her that I did not and would appreciate her nudging me in any direction that she thought might be helpful for finding financial support. Her response was, "Unfortunately, I don't really know. I just spend money, because I have money available from the State to execute projects." Inside I thought, "I wish I were in her situation – having money to spend on projects."

However, she was very helpful editing my proposal and essays, and I particularly appreciated how she helped me fine tune my evaluation sheet. Beyond that, I still had to find a way to fund the trip that would take my young son, two volunteers, three survivors, and myself to Nigeria.

An angel showed up in the form of a classmate, Sarah Leistico. Unlike many students who had approached me, Sarah was not asking me to share my personal and painful story for a human trafficking assignment; rather, she blew me away by saying that she was interested in helping me and my cause. One afternoon, over drinks and cookies at a local café, we discussed that the best way Sarah could help was to find ways to raise money for the trip. She took this suggestion seriously and got right on it, introducing me via email to Amber Hamm, the Student Senate President at Metropolitan State University. After meeting with Amber, we walked over to meet with the president of the University, Dr. Devinder Malhotra, Ph.D. From that vital discussion, I learned that I could apply for conference funds through the Student Senate to embark on the trip. However, I would not be able to bring along my entire group. Only my son, Brandt Schubbe (a student volunteer who worked with me on the proposal) and I would be heading to Nigeria.

Presenting the proposal was an hour long heated effort in front of the Student Senate, which fortunately ended in approval. I will forever be grateful to the members of the Metropolitan Student Senate. As if I had not had enough obstacles with this project and the funding for it, the System Office threw the Student Senate approval out the window when the employee in that office refused to sign off on it. The excuse was that Nigeria was a high-risk country. Luckily, President Malhotra reached out to the school's foundation, which then granted us the same amount. Although we were approved, we ran into another challenge. We had to use our own funds upfront and get reimbursed after the trip. Where was I supposed to get over $4000 in cash?

To meet this challenge, I am thankful to the board members of The Enitan Story, particularly, Annette Brandner, who I refer to graciously as Grandma. The board approved enough funding from the organization to pay not only for Schubbe and me, but also for my son — our youngest volunteer and a tremendous part of my story as a survivor. Grandma and her husband, Jim (Grandpa) donated additional funds and provided a loan for the remaining expenses.

We left MSP International Airport on Saturday, September 5, and arrived in Nigeria the following day. We were greeted at the airport by one of my brothers, Bolaji, his wife, Fadekemi, and my nieces. Fadekemi was our Nigerian representative and had been working day and night with me on this project. She met face-to-face with the U.S. Consulate Public Affairs Section staff, several influential individuals, and corporate organizations on our behalf. It was almost midnight by the time we reached Apartment Royale, the hotel where we would reside for our 12-day stay. It felt more similar to a small apartment than an actual hotel. We were treated to various dishes and soups that were provided by my friend, Ibukun Onasanya, who owned a catering business, Dunas Party Planner.

The following day, I held a live broadcast via the Periscope mobile app, to let people in the United States know that we had arrived safely. People joined from all over the world and I was impressed with the interested and engaged viewers. With no time to rest, the next day we headed for the headquarters of Nigeria's widest circulation daily newspaper, *The Nation*. There, I met with one of my editors from my time working at the paper, Mr. Lekan Otufodunrin, who had been following my story since 2009. The reporter who wrote the article about my situation in 2009 was also there to interview me for their YouTube channel. I reunited with some of my former editors and colleagues, and also connected with new ones.

On Tuesday, September 8, my tour fully kicked off with a press conference at the U.S. Consulate in Lagos. I couldn't be more thankful to Ms. Dehab Ghebread, Mrs. Joke Omotunde, Mr. Temitayo Famutimi, and Mr. Ayodele Durodola, for their unflinching support in coordinating national and international media to give the event full coverage. Once the press conference was over, I granted several one-on-one media interviews with Nigerian and foreign reporters. I am very grateful for all the media that gave the event the attention necessary to help educate Nigerian youth and prevent them from becoming victims of human trafficking.

The National Agency for the Prohibition of Trafficking in Persons (NAPTIP) also supported the events by showing up at the Consulate and the higher education institutions to speak to the attendees. I was invited to the Lagos Command Office, where Mr. Joseph Famakin, the Lagos Commander, welcomed us and granted an interview to talk about their work in Nigeria.

The Rotary Club of Akute, of which my uncle is a member, was also very supportive. They donated N25,000, an equivalent of $100 at the time. They invited me to speak at their monthly meeting and also attended the tour's grand finale event at the U.S. Consulate.

The tour of the higher education institutions took place over three days. My presentations were held in both classrooms and auditoriums, where sometimes community members were invited. At the end of my presentation at Yaba College of Technology, the students were instructed to write essays about my speech because they were from the mass communications department. Following each presentation, I distributed an evaluation form to the students to help me assess the impact of the project and also to note where I could make improvements. I was also interested in knowing if these events could be replicated in other higher education institutions in Nigeria, and in other countries around the world. I was pleasantly surprised and grateful at how the events were received. The support from the universities and polytechnic schools was outstanding and the responses from the students was encouraging. A whopping 772 participants out of 1000 returned their evaluation forms, and 98% asserted their willingness to host such an event in the future.

I returned from the trip to launch Students Against Abuse and Slavery International (SAASI) and hope to return and expand human trafficking prevention through awareness to other higher institutions within and outside of Nigeria. The entire trip, including interviews and presentations, was filmed and aired on the North Metro TV in Blaine, Minnesota and on the Imprisoned Show, and was also uploaded onto YouTube.

34

Top: Cross section of students at Lagos State Polytechnic, Ikorodu; Bottom: Left, Bukola Oriola presents copies of Imprisoned: The Travails of a Trafficked Victim to the Acting Consul General, the U.S. Consulate, Lagos, Dehab Ghebreab at a press conference held at the Public Affairs Section of the U.S. Consulate, Lagos; Middle, Bukola Oriola presents a Certificate of Appreciation to Acting Public Affairs Officer, Frank Sellin at the Grand Finale held at the Public Affairs Section of the U.S. Consulate, Lagos; Cross section of staff and students at Bells University, Lagos, Nigeria. Picture credit: Public Affairs Section of the U.S. Consulate, Lagos and The Enitan Story.

The three crew members that left Minnesota to Nigeria for Bringing the Story Back Home. Bukola Oriola and her son, Samuel, and The Enitan Story intern and Metropolitan State University graduate, Brandt Schubbe during the Grand Finale at the U.S. Consulate, Lagos.

Chapter 5

A White House Scam

I HAD just returned from Nigeria and was trying to settle in and adjust to the current time zone. It felt good to be home and back to my normal schedule and life. It was a needed break after fourteen straight days of little to no rest. I was happy that my son, Samuel, was back at school with his peers, after missing one week of school.

As I was still settling in, I received an email from the White House. The subject line was, "Time to talk?" I wondered, "Time to talk with who?" I pondered, "These scammers are at it again. This must be someone trying to scam me and pretend like he was contacting me from the White House." Without responding, I called one of my younger brothers, a computer engineer who had been working for IBM and also dealt with security issues. Once, in Nigeria, I stopped by his office and was not allowed to enter. Instead, he joined me outside and said I couldn't come in due to security reasons. So I knew he could probably help me figure out the legitimacy of the email. He instructed me to look in the details area and I told him that it still showed that it was from the White

House. Without mincing words, he said, "Then, it is from the White House."

My brother advised me to respond by asking the sender to ask his question. I did, and shortly after, I received a response that mentioned the U.S. Advisory Council on Human Trafficking and the sender was interested in speaking with me. I felt exhilarated because I knew for sure that I was the intended receiver of that email and that it was not a scam. I gave my phone number and shortly after, I received a call from the White House. The staff member asked if I was aware of HR 500, the Survivors of Human Trafficking Empowerment Act, which was passed into law in May 2015. Upon hearing that I was indeed aware of the Bill, he then asked if I would be interested in becoming a member of the U.S. Advisory Council on Human Trafficking. I answered, "I'm honored to be chosen and asked to serve." He then cautioned me not to disclose any of this discussion until the vetting process was complete and said, "We are moving things fast, and I need to speak to some other people that have been selected." He added, "You came highly recommended to us." In my head, I was astounded: "Me? Who recommended me?" It was a pleasant conversation and I told him how I had thought his email was a scam. He certainly was a comedian, saying, "Yes, by the way, give me your credit card number." Giggling, I replied, "Sorry, there's no money in it." He added, "Yes, that is what I tell the scammers. I tell them, have my card and good luck if you find any money." We ended the phone call, and a three-month anxiety started. Although I was told it would be a quick process, I was on pins and needles as I sat through interviews on the phone, answered emails and threw questions back and forth. Throughout the process, no detail was disclosed as to who was selected. Finally, two weeks before Christmas, on December 16, 2015, I received a congratulatory email that I had been selected to serve on the U.S. Advisory Council on Human Trafficking. The White House also published a list of the members on its website, entitled, "President Obama Announces More Key Administration Posts."

I was elated; I burst out crying. I cried for days. I cried in my room, on the road while driving or walking, at the store, at work, and at school. I just could not fathom how far I had come, despite the agony I had suffered for the first two years living in the United States. One day, my son was concerned and came into the room when I was crying. I had to explain to him that they were tears of joy, and that nothing was wrong with me. I explained the honor I was given and he was euphoric. He asked if he could tell his teacher at school, and I agreed. I wrote it on a piece of paper for him because the formal title was too long. The next day, I was pleasantly surprised by when I received an email from his teacher, Mrs. Pitzl, offered a congratulatory message:

"Hello Bukol[a], I saw the note you wrote for me about being appointed by Mr. Barak Obama to the U.S. Council. What a wonderful accomplishment. I just wanted to tell you that I am so happy for you! Congratulations. -- Diana."

The Nigerian community at home and through social media also went into a frenzy with news articles about my appointment. People began to write various homages to me. In fact, I was surprised to read some of the comments from my former colleagues. It was like watching a real life movie, but I was watching my own life story playing out in real time before my eyes. I received phone calls from all over the U.S. and Nigeria. Many sent me congratulatory emails, and others sent messages on Facebook or posted on my wall. I also had media interviews. Some who had been following my story called in to do a telephone interview. I also did a Skype interview with a reporter named Blessing, from Nigeria's *The Nation* newspaper.

In January 2016, the eleven council members were invited to the White House for inauguration during a meeting of President's Interagency Taskforce meeting. It was aired live, and I had the chance to take a selfie with the Secretary of State, John Kerry. Since then, we have been working with the Department of State's Trafficking in Person's office to write and submit our report to the federal government. Now, at the time of this writing, it has been ten months and we have finally finished work on our first report, with a launch date set for October 18, 2016. I look forward to making a positive impact that affects victims and survivors of human trafficking both within and outside the U.S.

Chapter 6

My Community of Support

D ESPITE THE fact that people have taken advantage of me as a result of my past experience, I have been very lucky to have a community of people who have been very supportive of my son, Samuel, and me. They are scattered all over the United States. Some are fellow survivors from Nigeria and other countries, some are advocates, and others are online acquaintances who have developed into colleagues, friends, and business associates. As a living survivor who works hard and still struggles financially, the supportive people who surround me give me hope and motivation to strive even harder until I reach my ultimate purpose. I wouldn't be where I am today without the help of such people behind the scenes. I am equally thankful to those who help take care of my son for days when I am traveling on behalf of human trafficking advocacy, as well as to those who invite him to play with their kids and who include him in their activities. I have other friends who cheer me up whenever I feel lonely and downcast. It's not easy living as a single mother. It is even more challenging to be living alone in a foreign land. I have made the community of people around me my immediate family.

I use them as a blanket to keep me warm during challenging times that feels like a snow blizzard.

I was on a difficult spiritual quest for over a year before discovering the United Methodist Church of Anoka. Before becoming a member four years ago, I used to attend church services online in my living room, waking up at 4:00 am to connect to the Sunday service in Nigeria. Occasionally, I'd connect to the weekly and special meetings held at other times. My journey reminds me of the story of Abraham, when God called him and asked him to leave his family and community to go to a land that He would show him. I am grateful to God for the Bible. One morning several years ago, I was praying when I received a scripture from the Bible. It was John 1:12 which states, "But as many as received him, to them gave He power to become the sons of God, even to them that believe on His name." (KJV). This scripture helped me realize that we are all children of God, regardless of our denomination, as long as we believe Jesus is the son of God. This enlightenment opened my eyes and I began my search immediately for a local church community. I then remembered that I had driven past a particular church for the past three years and decided to call them. On the following Sunday morning, I woke up my son and told him to get dressed for church. He questioned me because we had not attended church outside of our home for so long. I explained that we would be trying out a church in the neighborhood in the hopes that it may be a good fit for us. We arrived, sat through the service, and immediately afterwards, a woman named Winness, dressed in a blue choir robe, approached me. She greeted me kindly and noticed that I was attending her congregation's church for the first time. Upon learning that I was from Nigeria, she informed me that another Nigerian family also attended the church. I was happy to hear that. She said that they had not been in church for a while because they traveled. Seeing that I had a five-year-old with me, Winness introduced us to Emily, the Children's Ministry Director. Emily gave us a tour of the Sunday school and Samuel just fell in love with the place. He was so excited by all the toys and supplies that filled the classrooms. He had none of that at a prior Sunday School that he had attended.

We started attending that church every Sunday and Winness, my very first friend at the church, encouraged me to join the Bible class on Wednesday mornings. At first, I was quite surprised by the group. They were older than I had expected and Pastor Bill Eaves was the only man in attendance. I thought to myself, "Am I in the right Bible class?" By the end of the lesson, I knew that I was. I learned a lot from this group and also enjoyed their warm company. Many of the women have been very supportive of my advocacy effort and have helped me reach out to survivors of human trafficking and domestic violence through The Enitan

Story, a nonprofit organization that I founded in August 2013. They also provided funds for my trip to Nigeria.

I grew to feel very much at home in the church and chose to serve in the Children's Ministry. My church community really started to grow. I became close to Grandma Annette and Grandpa Jim. They are selfless people who are full of youthful energy for being in their seventies, have impressive memories of everyone's birthdays, and are gracious hosts for holidays and parties! I became close with Shakira, an Iraqi woman who attended church with her three children. Shakira's son, Ali, was the same age as Samuel, and the boys got along like brothers. They even attended the same elementary school before Shakira and the children moved away. I also befriended a Liberian woman, Bendu, who was in the Grandma and Grandpa church family circle, and her daughter. Another woman I was fortunate to meet and get to know was Grandma Comfort, a Nigerian. I encouraged her to join our church. Since then, we have looked out for one another. She was always supportive of my work, and when I was going to Nigeria, she came over to help me pack. I will forever be grateful to all of these people.

Top right and left picture, Bukola Oriola giving public presentation and Samuel helping with book signing. Bottom - Left, Becky Booker and Bukola Oriola, Right: Annette Brandner (Grandma and former board member) and Yvette Toko, The Enitan Story board chairman at The Enitan Story's office during bag party fundraiser for the Survivor Empowerment Sewing class.

Bukola Oriola's parents, Adesola and Sikiru Ogunmola

Chapter 7

Exploitation and Rebellion

I STARTED to become rebellious when I felt like I was being exploited. Heads of nonprofit organizations, founders or staff of other reputable organizations, and groups wanted me to share my story but were not willing to pay me for my time. The infuriating part was that they went home happy, raising money with my story or educating the community for state and federal grants. I was struggling to pay bills while my story was making money for other people. I remember a time when I had strep throat for three weeks, and having no health insurance, I was unable to seek medical attention. Luckily, after suffering with immense throat pain, I learned a sliding fee clinic where I could be treated at a low cost or for free. It was tough. This is one of the realities that informed the title of this book, *A Living Label*.

It was emotionally draining to see smiles on the faces of people who were benefiting financially from my story, while I struggled as a single mother with a son. I once attended a restaurant gathering of an organization that had used my story. As I sat quietly wondering how I was going to make ends meet, a well-intentioned

47

guest approached me cheerfully and said, "Thank you Bukola, I am a board member to X organization and your story has really helped us. We were able to raise money." I was perplexed. I didn't know whether to cry or scream. It was clear to a few guests that I was not my smiley self. But I remained silent. I felt sad. I felt voiceless. I felt powerless. My mental anguish made me feel as if I were tied to a rock and thrown to sink to the bottom of the sea.

After some long, hard thinking about this injustice, I found the courage to start using my voice. I realized that just like that woman in the restaurant, many people have good intentions, but they go about it the wrong way. I began to speak up against re-exploitation of survivors at events and at every opportunity I had. A staff member from one of the reputable national organizations approached me for a solution after a presentation that I had given which had noted this challenge. She explained that the grants her organization received only covered programs and staff salaries. Confidently, I advised her that her organization could seek support from the local community or philanthropists to pay survivors for their time.

I learned that I needed to seek out knowledge beyond the classroom if I were to take on this personal issue head first. I researched how to be a better speaker and how to present myself in a more professional way. I followed the examples of student leaders when I joined the Student Senate at Anoka Ramsey Community College. The more I learned, the higher my self-esteem grew. It became easier to say no without feeling guilty. I began to finally believe in my self-worth and I strived to become a professional.

I created a speaker request form to see if there was a conflict of interest, to find out if I would be paid, and to see if they would be willing to offer my book to the audience for purchase. I reclaimed my power and was now able to choose if I was willing to speak for free or not. While speaking without compensation is not always an issue for me, I do feel at times that I have been re-exploited when speaking for free. My speaker request form has helped me to work in a professional manner by declining speaking requests if I feel that they are not right. It gave me the fortitude to choose whether or not I wanted to donate my time or my story.

In April 2016, I was sitting on a panel with other survivors in a room filled with over 300 people to talk about the role of survivors in the anti-trafficking movement. Florrie was the moderator for that panel. This panel discussion was a part of the Freedom Network Conference where advocates, government officials, individuals, and groups gather to learn about partnering in and advancing the movement. While I was speaking, I told the crowd that I was not a commodity and, therefore, was not for sale.

I recall a time when I chose not to be re-exploited. I was asked to speak at an event that two hours from my home, to provide my biography, and to grant media interviews prior to the speaking engagement in order to increase attendance. After calling to inquire about compensation and being ignored for weeks, I learned that the organization was selling tickets and had designed a flyer displaying my name and picture without my consent. I was also told that I would not be paid any form of stipend or reimbursement for mileage. I declined speaking at this event. Another time that I felt re-exploited was when a university professor published a book which included an entire post from my website, again, without my consent. It would have at least been respectful if she had contacted me before publishing and selling my work. Like the woman in the restaurant, this professor had good intentions and was trying to illustrate what was going on in the movement and wanted to include survivor voices. In addition to my written words, she also interviewed survivors. However, I felt she committed one of the blunders she referred to in her book when she did not contact me before publishing my article in its entirety.

Survivors need to be respected as human beings who bring value to advocacy work. I always cite the Office for Victims of Crime (OVC) as a model of how an organization or individual should work with survivors. This federal agency and its staff give survivors due respect. Survivors are not treated like a number or a labeled item for sale at a store. Rather, this agency allows survivors to express themselves and provide valuable information to help the cause. I particularly appreciate that OVC refers to survivors as "subject matter experts" and not "survivors." They also regard survivors as consultants, and I am proud to be one of the OVC consultants who is treated with dignity rather than a wounded victim who has endured much suffering. Several other organizations that respect survivors as subject matter experts include the Alliance to End Slavery and Trafficking (ATEST), a project of Humanity United Action, and Freedom Network. It is not surprising because these organizations use the OVC model to engage survivors as consultants.

I am grateful to numerous other organizations and individuals who also respect my expertise as a survivor and respect me for who I am. They inquire about compensation and look to compromise whenever possible. One particular group I'd like to highlight is located in Grand Rapids, Minnesota, where I have developed trusted friendships. The group is in the process of raising funds to open its own safe house for girls called the Sweet Water Girls Ranch. When I was first invited to speak at their event some years ago, they completed my speaker's request form and politely answered my questions. When I eventually attended the event, they treated me like an important person in their midst. I wasn't portrayed to their audience as a survivor who had just come to tell her story, but rather as one who had come to enlighten the crowd about the issue of human trafficking in Minnesota. It is helpful to note that when inviting a survivor to speak at your event, present

the survivor as an expert with enormous personal value, and not just as a survivor to tell her story.

Bukola Oriola giving a presentation at various places across the country. Top: Left - the International Human Trafficking Institute in Atlanta, Georgia, 2015, Right - The Denver Anti-trafficking Alliance (DATA) first annual conference, Denver , Colorado, 2014; Bottom: Left – Trio Community Church, Mora, Minnesota, 2015, and Right – Calvary Baptist Church, Roseville, Minnesota, 2014.

Chapter 8

The Clouds Have Shadows

I WAS onboard a Delta flight from Minneapolis to Washington, D.C. as I gazed out my tiny window and noticed the movement of clouds beneath the plane. The sight of this took me right back to my geology class, and my imagination took over the gear stick in my brain. "The clouds are water moved by wind and have now formed ice. That's where rain comes from. The winds are in the stratosphere, and they are very cold," I remembered my instructor, Julie Maxine's words. I was still lost in imagination when it occurred to me to take a video of the moving clouds. I noticed something that I had never seen before. I could see the clouds' shadows. I was wondering, "Is this real, or am I seeing bushes?" The more I stared at this mystery, the more I was able to distinguish the bush from the clouds' shadows. I thought, "So clouds have shadows! Who would have thought that?" It was interesting to learn this new fact on my trip.

Just like the clouds' shadows, there are many victims and survivors who are unaccounted for in my Nigerian and African communities. Oftentimes, survivors like myself are invisible, despite their great effort to find solutions to the issue of human trafficking in their communities. It's worse in the minority-within-the-minority communities. For example, it is difficult to get statistics in communities where the culture forbids speaking out about exploitation or any kind of abuse. As a result of this stigma, many suffer in agony or die in silence. I still suffer the consequences of speaking out in my Nigerian community. Equally terrible is when provisions are made in advanced countries like the United States and services are available, these international communities are neglected because they are not regarded as vulnerable or high risk. I belong to one such community. Another very challenging issue is familial trafficking because it is difficult to detect when one family member is trafficking another relative. I have become aware that when statistics are not available for a particular community, it is important to recognize that the community is still highly vulnerable. It is like the story of the clouds and their shadows where it symbolizes how survivors do not have to be in the shadows. They can now be visible as professionals in the fight against human trafficking, using their experiences to become subject matter experts.

This trip to Washington, D.C. in 2014 was a dream come true, as I participated in the first White House Listening Session. The OVC invited several survivors, including myself, to develop a curriculum on professional development for survivors. It was a long year of "cooking food in the pot," but it's satisfying to see it come to fruition. Survivors worked with the Office for Victims of

Crime Training and Technical Assistance Center (OVCTTAC) to develop and facilitate this training. I was excited that the program was similar in style to my college instruction.

There were readings and assignments to complete via D2L Bright Space, an online learning platform, prior to face-to-face training. The training was launched with a webinar delivered by a fellow survivor. My head got swollen like cassava grain flakes in water (a dried grain staple in Nigeria that swells when water is added) when the biography of a survivor was read during the webinar. Her biography didn't read like a survivor or a victim, but like a professional with expertise to deliver. I joined the webinar by phone, and while the biography was being read, I thought, "Why didn't they have a survivor deliver this part of the training?" Then, I learned that it was indeed a survivor. I knew who she was, and I was tickled in my belly with happiness. As I mentioned earlier, the OVC treats survivors with dignity and respect as they collaborate and work with survivors and sets an example for many organizations as a model of excellence.

Bukola Oriola presenting at the OVC training in Virginia in June 2016

Chapter 9

Finding Bukola and My Mission

A S A victim-turned-advocate, I have been on a bumpy soul searching journey, filled with thorns and bristles. When I have the slightest inclination to stop or give up, a higher power arouses the doggedness in me to keep going, even when it means starting all over or taking a detour. This has happened on several occasions. When people ask, "How do you do all that you do?" I always answer, "I don't know how I do it." It's a sincere answer because I still surprise myself. It may sound weird, but it's the truth. My soulful journey revealed that my ultimate life goal is to empower others.

In my particular case, my mission is to empower survivors so they can achieve whatever they desire, regardless of their painful pasts. Also, I believe that the best revenge survivors can receive from their perpetrators is to prove them wrong. I have found this mantra to be very helpful: "I can do more than you can imagine to better myself and my life, regardless of what you think of or did to me." After much prayer and soul searching, I started a support group on Facebook. I took the leap after I was inspired by Christina, an event organizer from CAPI (a Minnesota based immigrant-led nonprofit organization), who, like so many others, suggested I start a support group for women. Around midnight on May 18, 2016. I posted a welcome video live on Facebook. After that first video, I had the urge to create weekly live videos.

Currently, this Facebook group, Stories of Enitan, includes both survivors and advocates and the weekly broadcast, called *Empower Monday!* airs every Monday at 5:00 AM CST. I was pleasantly surprised when I received a comment after my first broadcast from a group member who said she woke up feeling down, but after watching the video, she regained her energy to get up and keep going. After receiving several more positive comments, I was encouraged to continue my broadcast, despite the inconvenient time. Though I often don't go to bed until after midnight, I said to myself, "I will do it anyway and I will pray to God for grace and strength to keep going." It was after producing my first two episodes of *Empower Monday!* that the bud of a new idea grew in my mind. I envisioned starting a motivational show inviting inspiring speakers from around the world. I researched Google Hangouts on Air and started my first show on Monday, June 4, 2016. It was a 30-minute show to be broadcast right after *Empower Monday!* To my surprise, I found that people were interested in participating on my show. I hosted my first guest, Bob Abramson, a writer, lawyer, and business coach from Michigan who was looking for avenues to promote his upcoming book. Without thinking about any technical challenges, I quickly commented on his post that I was willing to host him on my online show, *Monday Motivation with Bukola*. Despite some technical glitches, the show was a success. Now, I have guests lined up and need to create an actual schedule for the broadcasts. Unfortunately, Google Hangouts on Air can no longer be accessed as easily so I modified *Monday Motivation with Bukola* to a recorded show which I now upload on Mondays.

Bukola Oriola

Bukola Oriola at the first Annual Report launch of the U.S. Advisory Council on Human Trafficking on October 18, 2016 in Washington D.C.

Picture Credit – Alswang Photography

Chapter 10

My Son, My Friend, and My Joy

MY SON, Samuel, has been a part of my story from victim to survivor to advocate. I wouldn't have received some of the services if it weren't for him in my life. He is my consolation for the agony that I had endured as a victim. He has continued to be a source of joy and inspiration to me as a survivor and advocate. He has gone with me to several presentations, volunteered at various events, and is now aware of anti-human trafficking efforts and their importance. He suffered with me, survived with me, and is now advocating with me. I will say that the best friend that I have had for almost a decade is Samuel. He is such a caring and understanding child who never worries me beyond trying to provide his daily bread. He's a child who is considerate enough to ask if I have enough money for him to buy a special toy or clothes. He understands that when I do have sufficient funds, I will spend it on him, but when I don't, we will manage with what we have, including wearing the same Halloween costume, for example, for three years in a row without complaining. I will say that I am a lucky mother.

Single parenting has been very challenging but it has been rewarding to be able to push through and accomplish the duties meant for two parents. I learn as much as I can from various sources online and offline. I accept support from friends when needed, especially when they babysit Samuel when I have to travel for days to speak about human trafficking. Before such trips, I make sure to cook some meals to store with my friends, Shakira or Emily, where he will be staying for a few days. Although he will eat the food they offer, having Mama's food is a way to help him cope when missing me. I make sure to call him daily when I am away to learn about his schoolwork and activities.

Growing up and seeing his mom work tirelessly, Samuel has grown interested in business ventures. In fact, he has asked me several times how to start his own business. He suggested selling T-shirts to make his own money. He attends an art school and frequently brings home artwork and paintings that he has created. Some of his artwork is even on sale on a website called *Artsonia*, which raises money for his school. After visiting the website and purchasing some of his artwork, I had an idea. I decided to create a bulletin board for him to proudly display his artwork. I rushed around to a variety of stores, purchasing foam, fabric, and other supplies necessary to make a unique board. It was fun choosing a fabric with baseball designs for him, just to make it a little kid-like. I even got Grandma Annette onboard to help with transporting some of the supplies. When I gathered all the items that I needed,

I set out to work right away. It literally took the whole day, and by the time I was putting the finishing touches on the board, the sun had already set and it was getting dark outside. After screwing the bulletin board to his bedroom wall, complete with *Samspiration* spelled out in butterfly-shaped art foam, we stood back and admired the colorful and cheerful art display board. I explained to Samuel that he could use the board for ideas or to post his artwork, and he was very excited. I went even further and built a website for him with the same name and we launched www.samspiration.com. On the website, he posts his artwork and also posts YouTube video art reviews.

I am impressed with Samuel in so many ways. Whenever I attend a parent teacher conference, the teachers always have positive comments about him. He blends in well with friends at school and is a team player. I tried to motivate him to read, so I promised to pay him one dollar weekly for reading. It worked but only for the weeks that I had money to pay. I also suggested to Samuel that he learn about Dave Ramsey's *Money Makeover* class at our church, and he took that plan and put it into action. He took three containers and labeled them for savings, spending, and giving. He uses his spending container for toys and birthday gifts for friends, the giving container for offerings in church, and the savings container to be put aside for future use. Although Samuel is only nine years old, I do respect his opinion and his suggestions whenever I make decisions that affect both of us. He is such an old soul. He reasons deeply and comes up with suggestions or ideas beyond his age.

Another important person in both my and Samuel's life is "Uncle Joe," a friend I who met at Anoka Ramsey Community College. He has been Sam's male role model since he was three years old. Uncle Joe supports Sam at various places, including at school. He even joined him on "Bring Your Dad or Male Role Model to School Day." Another important time when Uncle Joe showed up was on the first day of pre-school. Waiting at the bus stop in front of my hair braiding shop, a motorcycle stopped abruptly in front of us. The driver opened the covering of his helmet, and we both recognized who it was. With excitement, Samuel screamed, "Uncle Joe!" He parked and picked up Samuel to greet him warmly. He said he just came to support him on his first day at pre-school. Soon after Uncle Joe left the bus stop, the brown school bus with *Head Start* written on it pulled up in front of us. I helped Samuel onto the bus, put on his seat belt, stepped down from the bus, and watched it drive away. He loved school that whole first year but was disappointed when he entered kindergarten and realized there was no nap time and only a very short recess break. Though he complained in the typical manner of a 7 year old, he was also a very serious-minded fellow who took his school work seriously and did quite well academically.

Uncle Joe and his very kind family continue to be a great source of support for Samuel and me. They invite us to family gatherings and vacations. I remember one family vacation on a lake in Hayward, Wisconsin. Even though I couldn't swim, I went tubing in the lake and jumped off a pontoon. Luckily, Uncle Joe's sister, Aunty Mary, was there for me and helped me back to shore. It was a week filled with fun and joy, and Samuel and I loved it.

I feel relieved that despite the trauma and agony of human trafficking and domestic violence that we both endured during the youngest years of Samuel's life, he has grown to be a very good child, full of compassion, willing to help, and very understanding. He has learned to value volunteerism, raising money for a good cause, and advocacy.

Samuel's bulletin board and artwork from school and home.

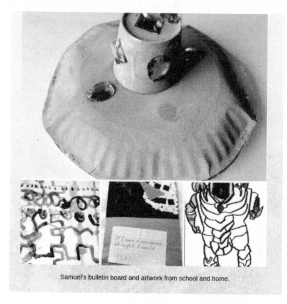

Samuel's bulletin board and artwork from school and home.

Chapter 11

Sudden New Battles

JUST WHEN I thought that I had left my agony behind, little did I know that I was going to be facing fresh battles, and reopening wounds that had begun healing as a victim of human trafficking and domestic violence. It was like watching a *Nollywood* (Nigeria produced) movie, when events that took place after the death of my ex-husband, who was my trafficker and abuser, unfolded before my eyes. For two and a half weeks, I was perplexed and scared as I relived the pain that I endured a decade ago. It was also the first time that rather than grieving for a passed one, I felt angry – very, very angry. Overshadowing that anger was fear, both for my life and for that of my child. Frightening thoughts raced through my now fragile mind, thoughts of others kidnapping my son and of being physically attacked by known or unknown persons. I became so depressed that it was hard to eat or even get out of bed in the morning. I was too weak to drive to work or even go grocery shopping. I got tired easily. It felt as if the sun stopped and the whole earth stood still. I hardly took a phone call or responded to an email. If I did respond, I made it brief and without a hint of my experience at the moment.

All of this emotional trauma began after having lunch with my friend, Becky. I first met Becky when I attended a fundraiser that I had organized to raise money to produce *Imprisoned Show*, a TV Show focused on human trafficking and domestic violence. Afterward, she invited me to speak and became a member of the Anoka County and Immigrant Refugee Asset Fund. She is one of those people in the community that has made a great impression upon me and has gained my trust by her genuine actions and her generosity. At lunch that day at Noodles and Company, she presented me with a gift of $1,000. She said, "I am not giving it to The Enitan Story, but to you, Bukola, to do whatever you like with it. God put it in my heart to give it to you because you are always running around to help others." Tears began to run down my cheeks.

On my way home that afternoon, I stopped at McDonalds to buy chicken nuggets and fries for Samuel. But what was supposed to be an evening of relaxation turned into a nightmare for me. I was about to take a short nap, when I saw that there was Facebook message on my phone. It was from a woman in the Nigerian community here in Minnesota who I had known through my ex-husband. The message read, "Please give me a call if you can. I have a very important message for you!" Though I rarely had any contact with this woman, I wasn't surprised to hear from her because various people contact me seeking help for themselves or for someone they know, ever since my story and my advocacy work has become public knowledge. Instead of receiving a message asking for help, I received the shock of my life. She said, "Brother Tade (my ex-husband, father of my son, *not his real name*) wants you to bring his son. The pastor is here. He wants you to bring his son to come and say goodbye to him. He just passed away this afternoon."

I didn't know what to make of what she had just told me. My head was spinning. I had been working without sleep for days prior to that on a website building training programs for sale online, and I wanted to take a short nap to reset my body and brain. The news that I heard through the phone left me confused and dumbfounded. On one hand, I felt a sigh of relief that I didn't have to fear Tade might find out where I lived, but almost instantly, anger rose out of my belly like a wave in the sea. I began to have flashbacks about the agony that I experienced by his hand as a victim of human trafficking and domestic violence as well as how I could not be granted justice at the court because I did not report the crime. I had always dreamed that my son would have the opportunity in his adult years to ask Tade his side of the story; now this was no longer possible. In the midst of these thoughts, I still had to pull myself together. I needed advice and called Emily, the Children's Ministry Director at my church, and told her what had happened. She advised me to tell Samuel and to ask if he would like to attend the funeral.

Once I finished telling Samuel what had happened, he fell silent for about a minute, and I saw him holding back tears. He succeeded in not crying, but he did express his sadness and told me that he would like to attend the funeral. That night, Emily and her son, Matthew, Samuel's friend, visited us. They stayed with us for a while, prayed with us, and asked many questions to which I had no answers. It had been almost a decade since we had had any contact with this man, so I didn't know anything about him from that point forward.

Samuel was in pain. He is a naturally quiet person, so it was harder to tell what he was going through. But he was not his usual self. He was quieter than usual and was not willing to socialize. He even refused to attend a favorite friend's birthday party at the last minute. For a mother, it was confusing and painful to witness. I started searching for a therapist for him. I wanted my son to be okay. I wanted him to be fine.

Moving forward, for my son's sake, I tried to find out the date and location of the funeral. Neither the pastor nor anyone else with the logistical information was willing to inform me, however. Instead, I received a call from the U.K from one of Tade's friends, who had heard that I was keeping the child away from his father's family. This is one of the barbaric attitudes some people hold in my culture. I wondered aloud why neither Tade nor his family came forward for almost 10 years, and why they would accuse me now, after his death, of keeping a child away from their family. I

70

thought about the agony some women experience when falsely accused of killing their husbands or ex-husbands when they pass away.

It was then that I realized we would need the protection of law enforcement to attend the funeral. While I was trying to help my son get closure, I was scared for my own life and safety and contacted the sheriff's office to see if I could get a police escort to attend the funeral here in Minnesota. I feared being hit or harassed by his friends or family members who might be present at the funeral. In the midst of this trauma, I woke up one day with a private comment on one of my YouTube videos accusing me of "killing an innocent soul." I forwarded the message to the Anoka County sheriff and he said that there was unfortunately not enough of a threat in the comment for them to take action, but that the local police would be on standby. This is one of the indirect threats that victims receive in my community. And that is the reason why many suffer in silence, because when they speak up, it is not only the perpetrator that they are up against. They are up against the whole community. We never did attended the funeral. Luckily, neither the lady who called, nor the pastor she claimed wanted me to bring the child to the hospital, ever provided any details about the funeral.

As a member of the U.S. Advisory Council on Human Trafficking, I reached out to President Barack Obama through a letter asking for his appearance with the Council at a town hall meeting to relay a message across sub-communities, like mine. (See a copy of my letter and the response from the White House scheduling office in the appendix.)

Making it a priority for Samuel to feel safe both physically and emotionally, I searched until I found a therapist that was a fit for both of us. My son's therapist shared with me that Samuel is unwilling to talk about grief for his late father and how this is not surprising since he had no contact when Tade was alive. She also noted that he may still be too young to process everything and may eventually start to process it as he matures over the years. Samuel created a safety plan with her, and that is paramount for us. I also got some online safety plans from my therapist for him.

I found my therapist to be very helpful, as I was able to express emotions that I had bottled up and finally felt that somebody could understand my perspective without judging me. I actually sensed that the mental agony I had been carrying around diminished. While working on this book, I started promoting it on Facebook and played music like a DJ. It was engaging and therapeutic for me, too. In fact, it led to another early morning show called "Morning Jamz with Bukola and You" at 6:00 AM CST on my Public Figure Facebook page. Since doing the *Jamz*, I have received both public and private comments and encouraging words from strangers. Some acknowledged and commended me for being the voice for the voiceless in the immigrant community.

In fact, a former police officer from South Africa, now residing in New Zealand, who works with immigrants, posted this message to me: "Your message is more powerful than you think. Just remember that survivors and victims are not always visible, but they are present and ready. Everywhere! And they need someone like you to speak for them. [....] As part of the police in SA [South Africa], domestic violence was enormous, also because of cultural beliefs, and it is almost impossible for victims to have any power to make a difference. They rely on people like you." Such comments like this give me the energy and motivation to carry on my advocacy work in the face of dire challenges.

Bukola Oriola

Chapter 12

Victim Advocacy and Survivor Empowerment

IN 2013, I decided to formalize my advocacy work by launching a nonprofit organization called The Enitan Story. Enitan means "someone with a story." It's a Yoruba name from my tribe in Nigeria. I chose this name to give assurance to survivors that someone shares a similar story and understands what they are going through. The mission of the organization is to advocate for victims and empower survivors of human trafficking and domestic violence. During this process, I consulted with legal counsels at the Legal Corp of Minnesota, I asked several trusted people to sit on the board, and I also registered for the Minnesota Council of Nonprofits' class on "How to Start a Successful Nonprofit."

With the help of the board, we registered The Enitan Story with the Minnesota Secretary of State's office, created our bylaws, developed a conflict of interest form, and launched the organization. It hasn't been easy running a nonprofit with virtually no guaranteed funding source other than generous donations from the public. However, we have still been able to support 19 survivors directly with emergency funding for rent, food, and basic needs, as well as immigration specific medical examination and skill training through our Survivor Empowerment Sewing Program (SESP).

It was also with the help of this organization that we reached over 20 million people during the *Bringing the Story Back Home* tour in Nigeria.

I find myself working as a case manager, making calls to victims and survivors, doing administrative work, responding to the board, and seeking support for the organization. A member from U.S. Senator Al Franken's (MN) community engagement staff visited our office and suggested that we look for volunteers through student internships. That was a wonderful idea and we now have one student from Mankato State University and four students from Metropolitan State University interning with us at The Enitan Story. I was happily surprised when these students completed their internship and chose to continue their volunteer work with our organization. Due to their extra hours and hard work, *Imprisoned Show* produced more episodes and articles on the website. We also have a student managing the Student Against Abuse and Slavery International (SAASI), a campaign of The Enitan Story, geared towards students for human trafficking prevention worldwide. SAASI was launched immediately upon our return from Nigeria to keep students engaged in human trafficking prevention and advocacy.

As a part of filling the gap in the services that are already provided in the community through The Enitan Story, I find great pleasure in helping others in my community. I volunteer by cooking at Alexandra House, the battered women's shelter where I received help almost a decade ago. I refer to Alexandra House as a family house, and I enjoy cooking for the women and children at the shelter. I bring along friends as volunteers, such as Khalilah and her group of helpers, who find assisting at the shelter to be a very rewarding experience. On other days, I get dirty in the soil, planting ethnic vegetables to support some of our clients.

Bukola Oriola

Chapter 13

A Message for All

MY MESSAGE to allies and the general public is simple – be caring, do your best to avoid stereotyped thinking when trying to help, and understand that survivors are human beings and not labeled items. I know for sure that there are individuals working hard to provide the best care for survivors, regarding emergency services or helping them to re-integrate for long term care. However, there are still huge gaps in the system. Gaps in messaging (for example, portraying human trafficking as solely sex trafficking), gaps in care services, cultural understanding, identification, survivor empowerment, and many other areas need to be acknowledged and addressed.

There needs to be greater awareness of the many different types of human trafficking. Many people equate the term "human trafficking" with sex trafficking. The public is much less aware of the presence of labor trafficking because these victims are unrepresented. Most messaging portrays labor trafficking as occurring only in certain industries such as farms, restaurants, hotels, and factories, but rarely mentions trafficking that occurs in homes. When it does come to light, we primarily only hear of cases involving nannies or domestic help. Cases like mine involving family members are rarely mentioned. Other victims of human trafficking include nurses, especially in the immigrant populations, whose spouses take their wages and are, therefore, their traffickers. There are international students who are exploited by their host families. These students are hardly acknowledged or represented when addressing the issues of labor trafficking. There are some trafficking cases that are treated strictly as domestic violence, because they involve only family members.

The federal government through the U.S. Department of Homeland Security must take a hard look at each of these categories of human trafficking. The agency can review the various U, T, and VAWA visa applications that have been approved in order to provide clear public messages that also address these kinds of situations in immigrant populations. There are survivors whose traffickers are not prosecuted, and those survivors need protection and support. A media outlet reached out to me recently to share my story but canceled once they learned that my trafficker had not been prosecuted. They feared being sued by him. This specific burden prevents many victims from speaking out or publicly sharing their stories even after they have received help. Though many would like to have a voice, they fear that their communities would turn against them or not believe them since their traffickers were not prosecuted.

Working with survivors can be mutually beneficial. I recommend that survivors create their own website and press kit or speaker's request form. I have created a booking form for myself which you can download and modify to suit your situation on my website, www.bukolaoriola.com. It is very helpful to the community when survivors are empowered to be independent and become taxpayers. It also helps to build and strengthen their self-esteem, which was taken away from them by their traffickers. For organizations or groups that might invite a survivor to speak who does not have a speaker's request form, you can also download and use the booking form on my website, www.bukolaoriola.com. Just modify it to suit your need and that of the survivor.

If you are a survivor and want to start your own website, you can do so for free or pay only $12 by using a Google domain. First open a Gmail account. If you already have a Gmail account, go to Blogger at http://www.blogger.com to start a blogspot, and you can modify it to look like a professional website. If you don't have the funding to hire a web developer, go to YouTube and watch videos on how to set up your website using Blogger. It's really easy and straight to the point. Having such a platform will really help you present yourself as a professional. You can also use it as a resource to offer solutions in the movement or to provide a safe place for fellow survivors to have a voice. I have also provided an eight-step plan that you can implement to turn your consultancy or career as a speaker into a business as a subject matter expert in Chapter 15.

Chapter 14

Becoming Hopeful After Trauma

L OOKING BACK at how far I have come, I know for sure that it's a miracle that I'm standing where I am today. When I think back to the time when I was a victim and I could not recognize myself in the mirror, I never knew that I would be able to look again in the mirror one day and recognize myself for who I really am. It is quite divine. I know that God is present with me all the time. I did not forsake my faith. I made the Bible one of my favorite books. It is so torn that I use tape to hold it together. I am not a religious fanatic, but I do believe in Jesus and trust Him through the Holy Spirit for help. Sometimes I have prayed before taking a step and I pray while I am in the midst of confusion or fear. This attitude of trust in God has been tremendously helpful in my journey and recovery.

I taught my son, Samuel, how to pray and rely on God for help whenever he is fearful. Sometimes, when he wakes up from a nightmare, I encourage him to say, "The Blood of Jesus," and to believe that he will be fine. Every night growing up, we sprinkled "the blood of Jesus," water from the tap, in all our rooms before going to bed. I have also raised Samuel to do the same. Whenever I am tired, I ask him to sprinkle "the blood of Jesus," and he does a good job of it. I watch him go into the kitchen to grab a bowl and fetch water in it, walk around the rooms and sprinkle, praying as he does.

At the office, I pray. In the car, I pray. This is a routine that I have become accustomed to. I also read motivational and self-help books. I have a list of books on my headboard that I am reading or planning to read. I have read some of them more than once. My favorite book is *The Power of Positive Thinking* by Norman Vincent Peale. Aside from reading the stories in books, I also look for actions to take. *Think and Grow Rich* by Napoleon Hill is another book that has been helpful to me in my business and in helping me develop leadership skills. There are many books that have had a great impact on my life in terms of focusing on being hopeful despite the trauma that I encountered. These books help train my mind to focus on the positive outcomes in my life, business, and leadership skills regardless of what the experience might entail.

I found out a strange thing recently. I was at the dentist for teeth cleaning and told her that one of my teeth would bleed whenever I brushed, so I tried to brush or floss gently. I asked the hygienist what cause this because it had been going on for a long time. She said that they couldn't find anything wrong, other than the fact that it could be as a result of trauma. I was shocked to learn that the trauma that I suffered might have also affected my teeth. I know that there is one healer – Jesus Christ. I have been praying ever since for healing in the affected tooth.

I am grateful for the therapists who have worked with me since I was diagnosed seven years ago with Post Traumatic Stress Disorder (PTSD). It has been very helpful, motivating, and hopeful for me to work as an advocate for other survivors. It is always very rewarding and meaningful to me when I have assisted in helping those who have been trafficked or abused transition from victim to survivor and get the help they need in and from the community.

Some of the news articles about Bukola Oriola in the ABC Newspapers Anoka County Shopper and Life, and North Metro TV website

Chapter 15

For Survivors Seeking to Start as a Consultant or Speaker

A S A survivor who has now become a consultant and an advocate, I have lived the reality of not knowing what to do or how to present myself as a consultant. There are so many questions to answer, from how to start a business to what to charge for my services. One thing that was helpful to me was that I already had a hair braiding business called Bukola Braiding and Beauty Supply, LLC, popularly called Bukola Braiding. I had registered it as an Assumed Name business until I met with a business lawyer who offered to organize my business as an LLC (Limited Liability Company). I developed the business beyond just hair braiding to training and helping others start their own businesses.

Starting as a consultant or speaker can feel daunting, especially if you have never been self-employed before. I have been in your position. When you have the necessary information, it will become less stressful. Below is an article entitled "How to Start Your Hair

Braiding Business in 8 Simple Steps" that I published on the Bukola Braiding website for those who want to start their own hair braiding business. I would like to note that starting any kind of business has similar steps. When you see yourself as someone in business, you can begin to think of yourself as a subject matter expert, which will help you overcome the fear of asking for money for your time. The steps below are for informational purposes only and not legal counsel. You should contact an attorney or your local Chamber of Commerce to learn more about legal obligations with your business.

1. Give Your Business a Name: Just like you have a name, your business needs its own name for the purpose of identification. Also, your business will be able to get its own social security number called a Tax ID for business purposes. You may want to choose a name that is easy to remember because it will help with marketing your business. You can use your birth name for your business, as I did with Bukola Braiding and Beauty Supply. As you can see, the name is quite long, so I usually just call it Bukola Braiding. If you use your full legal name, you may not need to register with the Secretary of State (SOS). When choosing a name, write down as many names that come to your mind and gradually narrow it down to the one or two that feel the most suitable for your business. Note that before you register your business, unless you

are using your full legal name, you will need to search to see if the name you have chosen is available. That is why it's a good idea to start out with several names. That way, if the name you want to register is not available, you can try the next one or tweak it a little bit.

2. Register Your Business Name: The second step is to register your business with the Secretary of State's office. You can start with an Assumed Name to become a Sole Proprietor. If you are starting small, then you will be fine with registering as Assumed Name. Otherwise, you can register as a Limited Liability Company (LLC) meaning that your company is standing by itself, and if the company gets sued, only the company's finances are used, and no personal property is affected. As a consultant just starting out, chances are slim that a lawsuit will target your property. Once you have submitted your business name application, you will receive a certificate of registration. You will need that certificate later.

3. Register Your Domain Name: The third step is to register your domain name. This means to register a name that you will use for your website. There are many options available for hosting your website, but I highly recommend self-hosting. The company I go with is called Blue Host. For less than $5 a month, you can register

your domain name. Usually, Blue Host will ask you to pay for about three years upfront, which is less than $200, and you will be glad you did. This way, you don't have to make monthly payments. You can have peace of mind about your website for the next three years. Domain name registration is similar to your business name registration with the Secretary of State. You have to do a name search to make sure it is available. I recommend that once you search the SOS's website to see that your name is available, go ahead and do the same with Blue Host to make sure it is available, so that your business name can match your website's URL. However, if the name you really like for your business is not available, you don't have to panic or worry, as you can also tweak it a little. For example, you can add a dash sign. The legal name for our nonprofit organization, for example, is The Enitan Story, but the website is enitan.org, and visitors can still find the organization. I mentioned Blogger earlier. Blogger will be your best bet, especially if you don't know much about website design and are not willing to spend a lot of money.

4. Set Up Social Network Pages: Starting a business in 2016 is vastly different from starting one ten years ago. Setting up social network pages will help market your consultancy or speaking business by promoting it to the

world at no initial cost to you. I recommend that you set up a fan page on Facebook. You create this from your existing Facebook personal account, but this page will strictly be for business. You publish only your business and business related posts on this page. Your posts for your personal friends can remain on your personal page. To set up a fan page, do a Google search to find out the steps. Next, set up a Twitter account if your business name is different from your legal name. You can do the same with Pinterest, YouTube and Google Plus. However, you can turn your Pinterest personal page into a business page. The most important thing to note is that when you start using your business social media pages, you need to eliminate all personal posts. That way, your business will look more professional and attract the targeted customers you need.

5. Get Your Business Tax ID: The fifth step is to get your business Tax ID. This is similar to the social security number for your business. Check with the IRS to see if you need a tax ID when you are using your legal name and operating as a sole proprietor since you have a social security number. You can call the IRS or go to their website, www.irs.gov, to apply. You will receive the number immediately and a few days later, you will receive

an official letter from the IRS showing that your business is registered with the agency.

6. Open a Bank Account: The sixth step is to go to your local bank and open up a business account. The reason is that you want to separate your personal account from your business account. When going to the bank, take the Secretary of State registration with you. You will present the certificate to the banker. If you don't have the IRS letter yet, you can just give them the number you were assigned online or on the phone. The minimum amount to open an account is usually $25. However, don't worry about the opening minimum. Be sure to ask upfront about any fees the bank charges and how to get those fees waived. If that bank does not have an option that sounds interesting to you, go to a different bank. For example, if you open with Wells Fargo, you will need to have an automatic transfer of $150 from your checking to savings every month to waive the fees.

7. Find a Location: This step is technically your first step. However, I have made it the seventh step here because you may be starting from your home. If you want to save on rent, the ideal thing to do is to start your business from home in order to save money. I recommend applying for a post office box so that you can use it for your business address.

8. Think and Take Notes: Set aside two hours a day to think and write down your ideas about your business. Make it part of your schedule to write at the same time each day. That way, you will become used to it. You can write in a notebook, or you can open a word document for writing. Just make sure that you have a folder named "Think and Take Notes." That way, you will start forming a disciplined attitude towards your business, which will help your productivity in the long run. Some notes will be actions to take immediately, goals for that week, that month, that year, etc. You can keep all your thinking notes in one place by signing up to use Trello at www.trello.com. It's really helpful for task management and also for setting goals. You can use it to work with team members as you grow as a business, or just use it to keep yourself on track.

Top: Bukola Braiding training in 2009. Bottom: Right – Braiding training in 2013, Middle – One-on-One braiding training, Left – model for braiding training in 2014.

Conclusion

I AM a survivor. My story is unique, and so is my role in the fight against human trafficking and domestic violence.

A Living Label is designed to explore some of my roles both as a survivor and an advocate. My vision with this book is to inspire other survivors to know that they have a voice and that their voice counts. Their voice has a value that is not found in any text or research. They are important and indispensable. Most of all, they are not commodities for sale or resale.

Unfortunately, people with good intentions sometimes re-exploit survivors without knowing it. I hope that this book will provide a basic guide for those who want to engage survivors in their advocacy work in a way that treats survivors with dignity and that their labors are appreciated and compensated. I hope that survivors and other allies can continue to work together in a way that is mutually beneficial.

I hope that all government agencies at every level of government within and outside the United States can embrace working with survivors as subject matter experts where they are adequately compensated for their labor. I hope that the U.S. government through the United States Agency for International Development (USAID) can work with its foreign embassies to begin a dialogue with those countries that receive grants from the agencies and to encourage them to include survivors' voices in their policies to better serve the needs of survivors right in their own country.

My college essays - edited

IN CHAPTER 2, I promised to share some of my college essays with you. I have selected three of such essays because they are writing on the issue of human trafficking and domestic violence. One was about introducing ethnic food at the battered women shelter so that their population from other cultures can enjoy comfort food, especially eating the food that they are familiar with from their home country. Another essay focused on a woman who made a great impact on my life as a survivor and business woman. She helped me expand my hair braiding business and even nominated me for an award which I received. The third essay focused on how I helped one woman, a client, get help.

Bukola Oriola in the library at Anoka Ramsey Community College, Coon Rapids, Minnesota

"It Feels Like Yesterday"

IT FEELS like yesterday. It's been six years already. How time flies! Where has the time gone to? On October 16, 2013, it will be exactly six years since I began a journey into freedom with my son as a survivor. We are, indeed, both survivors. I am a survivor of domestic abuse; I am a survivor of human trafficking. You have no idea what it feels like to be imprisoned until you lose your freedom for a moment. You have no clue what it means to crave food as a pregnant woman, but not be able to eat, not because there is no food, but because you are being tortured for a crime being committed against you. You cannot fathom working while someone else is collecting the money. I have lived it. I have survived it. I am a survivor.

According to various sources, one in four women experience domestic abuse in their lifetime. Eighty-five percent of abuse occurs by an intimate partner. The rate of domestic abuse is high where "estimates range from 960,000 incidents of violence against a current or former spouse, boyfriend, or girlfriend to three million women who are physically abused by their husband or boyfriend per year," (Domestic Violence Resource Center). Human trafficking, on the other hand, is higher, being described as the third largest crime in the world, next to trafficking of firearms and drugs. Human trafficking can happen as a result of fraud, force, or

99

coercion. Additionally, human trafficking can occur not only among strangers, but also among family members. It is the modern day slavery. It is interesting to find out that sometimes, human trafficking can be hiding under domestic abuse. It takes further investigation to reach this conclusion.

Since 2009 when I decided to go public by putting my face to my story, it has been both rewarding and fulfilling for me. Some victims are now able to identify themselves; others who come in contact with victims are helping victims to reach out for help. The first person who reached out to me for help was one of my hair braiding customers, Hope (name withheld). It was about six o'clock in the morning. I was in the kitchen getting ready to prepare breakfast for my son, and before heading out to church for the Sunday morning service, I went to the kitchen and opened the fridge thinking, "What am I going to prepare this morning?" As usual, I bent down a little bit with my right hand holding the door to the fridge; and my eyes scanning through the three layers in the fridge holding pots of soup, plastic containers of cooked food, vegetables, eggs, and leftovers, to get an idea of what to prepare that morning.

I had yet to decide when my cell phone rang. "It's early! Who could be calling at this time of the morning?" I thought. I closed the fridge and went for the phone to unplug it from the socket where I left it to charge overnight. When I reached the phone and saw the caller ID, I was happy that my prayer had been answered.

I had just barely finished praying and went into the kitchen to get ready for church, and a customer is calling already? Every day, I pray for my customers; more so, I pray that they call to make hair braiding appointments. Well, not so fast. It was a prayer answered, but not for hair braiding. A victim of human trafficking needed help. When I answered the phone, "Hello, good morning, Hope," the response I received was, "Bukola, those people that helped you, can they help me?" with a despondent voice. For a minute, I forgot that I was looking for food in the fridge; I concentrated on the telephone conversation. Meanwhile, all kinds of thoughts flashed through my mind simultaneously: "So, some of my customers are victims of domestic abuse; some are victims of human trafficking; some are not safe at home. It was a good idea that they read my book for free or bought it at the shop." I controlled my thoughts to come back to the present conversation and said, "Yes, they can help you. The help is not only for Bukola, but for everyone who needs help." I told her, "Hang on, let me look for the number."

While she was waiting on the other end of the phone, I reached into my contact list to look for the number of the host of the support group for Immigrant Women and Refugees where I had been helped as a foreign-born victim. I knew she would be the best first contact for Hope. She worked at the Home Free shelter for battered women in Plymouth, the same city where Hope resided. "Hello" I said. Hope said, "Hello." "Okay, take down this number and call now," I said. After dictating the number to her, I assured her that she would be fine. When the call ended, I felt like I had just won a battle. The reason I published my book had come to fruition. Apparently, Hope was one of my customers who had bought and read my book when it was published in 2009. She never said anything to me other than, once, she recommended that I should have my book in book clubs and book shops around the Twin Cities.

Hope called the number I had given to her, and she moved to the shelter with her twins. Her husband, who was the culprit, had run back to their home country in the southern part of Africa. I did not ask for the details of her story other than sending her to the right place; however, I continued to follow-up with her by calling and checking to see how she and her kids were doing. I supported her in little ways that I could, like braiding her hair for less, and one time, I braided her daughter's hair for free. I offered words of encouragement as she went through the process of restoration. For a foreign-born victim of human trafficking, it is a very long process because one of the needs is getting a status to remain and work in the United States legally. It is therefore very challenging for someone with two kids, when there are barely any means of income for survival. Thank God for the shelter, where basic needs are provided, but there is a distinct difference between earning an income to cater to yourself and your children, and surviving with the help of a shelter.

Human trafficking is becoming a prevalent crime around the world. The United Nations estimates that over two million people are being trafficked around the world. In fact, two years ago, President Barack Obama declared the month of January Human Trafficking Awareness Month to create awareness and prevent the crime in the United States. In the past few years, many non-profits organizations have sprung up to advocate, rescue, or restore victims of human trafficking. The media are also paying attention to the issues of human trafficking, with reports flooding the various media from print to online, sensitizing the community to the heinous crime. Hope is just one of many who have reached out to me for help since 2009. I have recorded victims reaching out for help from outside of Minnesota. I have seen victims reaching out for help among students at Anoka Ramsey. A victim reached out at Scholastic University in St. Paul after I shared my story.

It's only been six years, and I am happy at how far I have gone with my advocacy efforts. I am happy to see others reach out for help. Currently, a victim of domestic abuse all the way in Georgia is getting help because he was referred to me. Right now, I feel like no matter how dark the night might be, the sky will show its brightness in the morning, with or without the sun.

Works Cited:

Domestic Violence Resource Center. Domestic Violence Resource Center. n.d. Web. 6 Oct. 2013

"Not The Birthday Present"

I T WAS October 30, 2013. My friend Joe woke me up with a telephone call singing, "Happy birthday to you…" I laughed, and said, "What a nice way to wake up. Thank you for the birthday song." Then, he replied, "How does it feel to be twenty-nine years old?" I said, "Not twenty-nine, but nineteen years old." We both laughed and he said, "Your voice cracks from sleep." I said, "Yes, because I am just waking up." After a little conversation, he asked about my son, Sam, and he said, "I better leave you to go get Sam ready for school." As soon as he hung up, I received an email notification on my phone. When I checked, it was an email from Joe's brother and his family wishing me happy birthday. I quickly replied with a thank you note and jumped out of bed. I went to Sam's room to wake him up to get ready for school.

I have a long day ahead of me, I thought. It's Wednesday, and therefore, I have to head for Cambridge after dropping Sam off at school to tutor for two hours. I was running late, so my preparation speed was almost like the speed on the light. I kissed Sam goodbye as usual before he alighted from the back of the car to join the assembly line in front of his school. Proceeding to Cambridge, I drove as fast as I could, checking my speed limit, and slowing down, sometimes, to avoid being pulled over by the police. I listened to the morning show on Minnesota Public Radio. The topic was about a book on the Republican and Democrat values, and why young Republicans are being lost to the democrat's camp. It was not my favorite topic, but I listened anyway.

It was about 3:50 in the afternoon and I was pulling into the parking lot at the Coon Rapids campus of the Anoka Ramsey Community College for a Punctuation Workshop that started at 4:00 p.m. Meanwhile, I had just ended a telephone call with a friend who was wishing me a happy birthday. We had cracked jokes and laughed so hard that my ribs hurt. She had a class that night; otherwise, she would have taken me out for dinner to celebrate my birthday. "I would have loved to see you in your pink dress and danced while we had a fun night but I am sorry, I have a class," she said. I told her, "Don't worry, there would be many more times to celebrate."

"By the way, how old are you?" she asked.

"I am nineteen years old," I said.

"No, I don't think so," she replied.

"Yes, I am nineteen," I insisted.

"Well, I know you are joking with me. Anyway, happy birthday! I hope we can get together when we both have the time to celebrate your birthday," she said. Yes, I was joking with her about my age. I was just trying to be humorous.

I was still smiling and checking my messages really quickly before running into the building for the workshop when my phone rang. I recognized the number. It was a common number that appeared on the caller ID when a call came in from the Anoka County offices. I thought it was my case worker, with whom I was supposed to make an appointment to meet in November. However, the call was not from her; instead, it was from the Anoka County Community Action Program (ACCAP) office, which was also in the Anoka County offices. It was Judy Bond, the boss to Joan Karow, my savings account coordinator from the Family Asset for Independence in Minnesota (FAIM). I was expecting to hear, "You need to deposit the remaining amount on your FAIM account," instead, I heard, "I didn't want to send you an email and I thought I should call you. Joan passed away. She passed away on Monday." My response was a loud, "Eh!" Then, I paused for a moment. I was in shock. Judy kept talking, but I was lost. I could not comprehend her. When I could speak, in a brittle voice, I asked, "Can I call you back, please?" She said, "Yes." I dropped the phone in the cup holder between the driver and passenger's seats without hanging up. I cried my eyes out for about thirty-five to forty minutes. The car engine was running, the radio was going, I was sweating profusely and crying like a baby.

I sobbed very hard, gasped, and was broken. Even though I was a client to Joan, I had formed a bond with her in the three years that I knew her. She was pleasant, friendly, and very kind. She was a trustworthy person. She always looked out for me. When she enrolled me for the first time for the FAIM program, I did not have my permanent resident card but a work authorization. She said to me, "Never mind, I will put your work authorization on file and you will be fine." In fact, before the program started, she had put me on the waiting list, and as soon as the program started, she called me to come for enrollment at her office. With the FAIM savings, where every dollar was matched with three, I saved for two years, and was able to relocate my shop from a 132 square foot space in Anoka city to an office with 400 square feet in Spring Lake Park. During the grand opening in February 2011, Joan was the first person to show up and the last person to leave. She nominated me for the FAIM state award and I won the Outstanding Saver's Award in the Business Category. She helped me to participate in the ACCAP spring sale, where she set me up in a choice spot. In fact, other vendors could not hide their envy for my taking the choicest spot. They kept making side comments, but Joan came to check on me several times and told me not to worry. She even bought a scarf from me. Last year, I hosted a fundraiser for the kids at Alexandra House to help them with school supplies, and again, Joan was there to show her full support.

Around August last year, she had called to check on me to see how I was doing with business. I told her that I was still having challenges, and she said,

"Bukola, you can participate in the savings program again. Did I tell you that you can do it twice?"

"No," I said.

"Sorry, it was my fault; I thought I had told you that you have a second chance with the program. Whenever, you have the time, come to the office and we can get you started," she said.

I told her, "I will be coming right away."

Luckily, my shop was not far away from her office, so I drove to her office to take advantage of the second chance to give my business a boost. I told her,

"This time, I would like to use the money for marketing because I think that will help to bring more customers into the shop."

She said, "That would be a good idea. You already know how the program works; just deposit your forty dollars a month and you can take half out in six months."

Then, I said, "I think I will wait for a year to plan the proper marketing strategy."

She agreed with me and I enrolled again. However, in December, I just stopped by at her office as I usually did whenever I was in the building. I was like the "stalker" client. She welcomed me whenever I stopped by without an appointment. She talked with me, advised me, and showed me opportunities that might be available. That day, she did not take me back to her office; instead she used a little room beside the reception to talk with me. She told me she was not feeling well. "They found a tumor in my spine, and they were not sure whether to do surgery or not. But now, it is bothering me so much because I cannot sit for long, so I have to go in for surgery. I will be back by February," she said. "How will I be able to communicate with you," I asked. "Do you have my cell phone number?" She asked. "No," I replied. She gave me her cell phone number and said "You can call me any time." I asked, "Is there anything I can help you with?" Who will stay with you? Who will help you around the house?" I just kept asking several questions to see how I could be of help to my helper. She said, "Don't worry, I have people that will help. Moreover, there is not much to do. But you can call me."

I called after some weeks and left a message on her phone, but when she returned my call, she left a message on my phone because I missed her call. I felt sad that I missed her call, and I called her back, but there was no response, so I left a message. I left several messages. I became worried when she did not return to work in February. I kept calling until luck was on my side. I was driving one day to Wells Fargo when she came to my mind and I decided to call her. Luckily, she picked the phone. At first I wasn't sure if she was the one, but then, I recognized her voice. I asked, "How are you doing?" She said, "Not so good. I am at the cancer unit at the Methodist hospital in Rochester." I told her, "You will be fine because we are praying for you." She replied, "Please, pray. I need it." Then I asked, "Can I come and visit you?" She said, "They don't allow visitors here but your prayers will be good, too." At that point, I had driven to the drive through ATM machine for a quick transaction. I told her I will be praying for her. I asked for prayer requests on her behalf at my church, and they prayed. I prayed and trusted God for the restoration of her health.

Since Joan left on sick leave, Judy had been standing in for her. She gave me feedback sometimes, and I was very happy when she wrote me an email around the end of August that Joan was doing much better. I was hoping she would resume work soon. Two weeks before, when I received my FAIM account statement from Judy, I asked about Joan and she replied, "I have not heard from her in a while, but I will find out and let you know." The last message I was expecting was the news about Joan's death. Joan was like a mother to me. She passed away two days before my birthday, very close to anniversary of my own mother's death. My mother had passed away the day before my birthday in October of 1998. Joan was buried on November 2, 2013; my mother had been buried on the same date in 1998. I was invited home from college in Nigeria when my mother passed away; I received the news about Joan's passing in college. It was double tragedy for me. I drove to Rochester on Saturday, November 2, for the showing and burial ceremony for Joan. Joan was cremated, so I did not see her beautiful face, but I was able to touch her box of ashes, and said my silent prayers sobbing.

At the burial, I was the only black person in the crowd. When I got to the Ranfranz & Vine Funeral Home, the venue of the ceremony, I passed by some visitors outside and went through the white French doors into a waiting area. I asked two men in black suits, "Where is the lying in state?" They did not understand what I meant. I realized that "lying in state" was not what Judy had told me. She had said, "The viewing is from 1:00 p.m. to 2:00 p.m." when I called a day after she broke the news to me. So, I said, "I mean the viewing," then they pointed to another room where people had gathered. I thought there was a line and stood behind some people. Two other people joined me and someone said, "There is no line, you can just go in." We went in, and there was a small line by the bouquet of pretty flowers with a table in the middle with Joan's box of ashes, picture, family picture, a basket of scarves, with the sign holding Joan's picture saying, "Joan was a lover of scarves, so you can take one of her scarves." When I got to that table, I saw the box. It was my first time seeing someone's box of ashes. Her name was inscribed on a copper plate attached to the box. Still, I wasn't sure; so I asked the man in front of me, "Is this Joan's ashes?" I had seen him touch it and say a silent prayer. He said, "Yes, that is Joan." While I was sobbing and praying, a lady in front of him said to me, "Are you the lady with the braiding shop?" I said, "Yes," surprised that anybody would recognize me at an event where I was obviously the different person in the crowd. Then she said, "Joan said a lot about you." I thought, "Wow!" She asked, "Do you know any of the family?" I replied, "No." She said, "Let me introduce you to Joan's baby sister, Jody." She did, and I said to Jody, "Joan was a great loss to me. I hope her soul rests in peace." She hugged me and I continued, "Can I make a request?" She said, "Yes." She held me close so I could speak in her ear and I said, "I will like to start a savings fund in Joan's name for survivors of human trafficking." She said, "That will be great. Thank you."

Shortly afterwards, I took a blue winter scarf from the basket, and we went in for the burial ceremony. The funeral ceremony began. Then, it was time for friends and family to have their free time to share their testimonies about Joan. I broke the thirty second silence by raising my hands to share my testimony with uncontrollable tears. Then, the next person who spoke after me said, "If it consoles that lady in any way, I would like to say that Joan talked about her to us a lot." Directing the talk to me, she said, "Joan was proud of you. We didn't know your name, but we knew you as the lady with the braiding shop." Then another person said the same thing, and another person said a similar thing. I entered the room thinking nobody knew me, but almost half of the room had known me before meeting me. Everybody's testimony about Joan was the same: she was kind, loving, and even when she was in pain, she was always smiling and never complaining. In her memorial pamphlet entitled "Afterglow," Joan wrote, "I'd like the tears of those who grieve to dry before the sun of happy memories that I leave behind when day is done." Joan was a happy woman, even in death. I will forever cherish her in my heart.

"Lack of African Ethnic Food at Alexandra House"

Abstract

There is lack of ethnic food at Alexandra House in Blaine, Minnesota. Alexandra House should serve African ethnic food once a week, starting from fall, 2013, to help African immigrant women that seek refuge at the shelter have access to familiar food for comfort. The state of Minnesota has become more diverse in the past 20 years; more Africans migrate to the Twin Cities and resettle in the suburbs. Alexandra House needs to change with the state's cultural diversity trend to be able to provide proper service, especially in terms of diet to African women. The shelter has increased the number of cooking staff; therefore, it is perfect timing to include an African menu weekly. The shelter staff will receive free training with the help of African women at the shelter to cook nutritious menus. African foods are nutritious and healthy; therefore, the shelter will still be serving menus that are in accordance to the state's health and safety menu code.

IMAGINE GOING through severe agony or any kind of torture such as domestic abuse, human trafficking, or sexual assault from the hands of a known person or a total stranger. Imagine enduring hunger, in addition to the physical, psychological, mental and emotional trauma a person has suffered, only to find out that the safe place for refuge does not have a menu

115

that provides foods that are familiar. Such is the case for many African immigrant women who are running away from their abusers and/or traffickers, to seek refuge at the Alexandra House in Blaine, Minnesota - the only battered women's shelter in Anoka County. As an African immigrant survivor of domestic abuse and human trafficking with firsthand experience, I was unable to eat the foods provided by Alexandra House because they were not familiar. It was not enough for me to be in a safe place; it was also very important for me to eat familiar foods for my total recovery. Alexandra House cooks should serve African ethnic food once a week, starting in the fall of 2013, so that African immigrant women who are seeking refuge at the shelter can eat familiar foods to feel more comfortable in their new place of refuge. This will promote cultural exchange among the women and staff of Alexandra House, while the children will learn to embrace other cultures.

As the only shelter for battered women in the northern suburb of the Twin Cities, Alexandra House is host to many women victims of domestic violence and their children from this area and other parts of the state. Even though women from within and outside of Minnesota can seek refuge at the facility, the majority of its clients are from Anoka County. According to the 2011 Annual Report of Alexandra House, it is the largest provider for domestic abuse and sexual assault victims in the state of Minnesota, and has worked with over 3000 clients, a 26 percent increase from 2010 and 2009 (Alexandra House). Since it is the only battered women shelter in Anoka County, 80 percent of its clients are residents of the county. The shelter received over 13,000 calls on its 24 hour crisis line during these years (Alexandra House). Furthermore, news reports and the state census have recorded a great increase in the migration of immigrants to Minnesota. More and more foreigners, including Africans, are making Minnesota their home in the past 20 years. "The number of Minnesota residents who were born in Africa increased six-fold in the 1990s, according to the latest round of US census data....Minnesota had about 4,800 in 1990 and 34,000 in 2000," (Leslie and Writer).

In addition, a majority of minority people, including African refugees, are relocating to the suburban areas that used to be populated almost exclusively with white people. In a *Star Tribune* report, immigration expert Katherine Fennelly of the University of Minnesota suggested that some of the reasons the change is happening is due to the need for parents with young kids to live in a safe neighborhood with good schools (Peterson). The 2011 United States Census Bureau data also showed that Anoka County makes up one seventh of the entire population in the State of Minnesota, with over three hundred thousand people living in the county. Among these, seven percent are foreign born, while 2.4 percent report two or more races (Bureau). This evidence showed that there is a need for Alexandra House to modify its services to better serve women from other races, including African. Providing familiar foods to these women will go a long way to help their emotional, psychological, physical and mental recovery, especially when they have to stay at the shelter for longer periods of time. Program supervisor, Betty Balan stated that immigrants stay at the shelter "anywhere from three months to a year. We keep them until they can stand on their feet because they have more barriers," (Balan). A woman who has endured despicable agony needs to have the right diet, especially a familiar one, to accelerate her total recovery. This will also be of great benefit to the staff, who will not only serve foreign food, but learn ways of cooking delicious and healthy meals in different ways.

It is stressful enough to have been in a situation that led a woman and her children to the shelter. Not having access to familiar food in a place where the woman will be staying for an unknown period of time can even be more stressful. Masataka Nuokawa, a psychology professor at Anoka Ramsey Community College, also noted that it is stressful for immigrants living in the United States to eat unfamiliar foods when they are not in any kind of abusive situation, let alone people who are already stressed (Nunokawa). Having familiar food in addition to other programs provided by the shelter will help African immigrant women cope and heal faster during such periods. Rita Apaloo, a leader in the African community and founder of African Women Connect (AWC), a networking group for African women in the Twin Cities, also stressed the importance of providing ethnic foods at the shelter. According to her, being provided with familiar food during a stressful period would give women at the shelter comfort (Apaloo). Serving African ethnic food once a week will help African immigrant women seeking refuge at Alexandra House enjoy complete comfort during their transition into a safer environment as they move forward with their lives.

One main solution is to begin the process by introducing some of the staple foods like rice, cassava grains, fufu, and gari served with vegetable soup or stew. In fact, yams, potatoes, and corn flour are familiar to these ethnic groups. One mile away from the shelter is an Asian food market where African foods and ingredients can be purchased. After all, a Minnesotan can experience "Africa without leaving Minnesota [by just visiting the] Somali mall in Minneapolis or [the] African Shopping center in St. Paul" (Leslie and Writer). The shelter cook can use the help of the African residents for both purchasing the right ingredients and cooking in the kitchen. Also, the shelter can get help through volunteers in the African community to accomplish this task. Serving African ethnic food at Alexandra House will accelerate the healing process of the African immigrants at the shelter, while the staff, other women, and their children would benefit from trying healthy foods from a continent other than theirs. Rice, for example, is a global cuisine, and it would pair well with fruits, vegetables, meat, fish, chicken, eggs and other protein foods

(Federation, USA Rice). The kitchen staff would find it very helpful and educating for the women to go shopping with them at the grocery stores. For example, there are various kinds of rice, e.g., Jasmine, Uncle Bens, Minute, Parboiled, and so on. As a result, there are various ways of preparing these different kinds of rice to make it cook right. The African women would be handy to guide the staff on the right purchase and proper cooking in order to provide enjoyable meals.

Although, women from other ethnic groups might not find African food palatable, it would give them a chance to feel some of the distaste the African women experience when they have to eat American foods that they are not familiar with. The shelter provides sandwiches, yogurt, fruits and milk on the side for women and children at all times. The women who would not like to eat the African dish for whatever reasons could have peanut butter and jelly, turkey, or chicken sandwiches, in addition to yogurt and fruits. However, preparing some of the universal dishes like rice, served with vegetables and meat, will help other ethnic groups tolerate the food better. As someone who grew up in an African country, I never had dessert of pie or pastry like it is in the American culture; I usually had seasonal fruits as dessert. This is an added advantage to the women to enable them to eat healthy foods while staying at the shelter. Whenever an African dish is served, a bowl of fruit could compliment it for dessert, instead of sugary pastries.

Furthermore, the children from other races will learn to embrace other cultures from a young age. For example, when they go to school and see a child with a food they are not familiar with, it would not be totally strange to them; rather, they might be curious to know about the food. It would even be better when such food is what they had tried at the shelter; they would learn to appreciate a different culture and tradition, and it would further promote diversity and "a higher level of acceptance when people understand and appreciate other cultures," (Mamaril). Also, it is not just satisfying the African women but other ethnic groups as well. This is a perfect opportunity for Alexandra House to expand its cooking to include foods from the various regions of the world and serving African ethnic food would only be once a week. The shelter could use this as a ground to explore common food items from various ethnic groups and combine them into one dish for the women to feel some sense of belonging.

Another problem envisaged would be lack of experience of shelter cooks, which might result in improper cooking. However, this is a problem that would be easily tackled with the help of the women; it would be of immense benefit to the cooks to get free culinary training from the African women at the shelter. In the African culture, women are trained to cook or lend a helping hand in the kitchen from a very young age. Giving the women the opportunity to help staff in the kitchen would serve as another

121

process of feeling more relaxed; more so, it will further enhance their recovery process. Money is another issue in every program at the shelter, including the introduction of new foods in the menu; however, the shelter program supervisor, Balan agreed that it is not expensive to make ethnic food. "We would love to make different dishes and mix many different cultural foods together. We can get the Minnesotan dish, for example, and turn it into something totally different," (Balan). This will further strengthen the cultural exchange among the women, their children and the Alexandra House staff.

An alternative solution would be for the shelter to make a recipe book with the help of current or former African clients, and volunteers or staff. In fact, six ethnic groups work at the shelter, (Balan), therefore, it is a diverse place where food can also be diverse. Balan rejected the idea of making a recipe book; however, the shelter cooks could continue to explore the internet as they have always done occasionally to prepare ethnic foods. In addition, the women could continue to help the staff in the cooking process to ensure the foods taste like they were made in Africa. Besides, Alexandra House could lend some ideas from other organizations such as the SOS Children's Village, United States, where they have put together recipes from 113 countries around the world, including Africa to help the children at the orphanage adapt properly. African cuisines are diverse, comprising of locally grown vegetables, fruits, grains, and meat (USA, SOS). Alexandra House would be proud to exhibit itself as a shelter with program diversity, thereby improving its portfolio among other battered women shelter in Minnesota. Likewise, it would benefit greatly from this situation by generating revenue from the recipe book through a fundraiser. The recipe book would serve as a win-win venture where the shelter staff can look into for recipes for the women at the shelter, both African and other races, and a fundraiser tool, since the shelter relies solely on public and government donations to thrive. The cooking staff will have a cheap opportunity to boost their resumes as international chefs, which will carry them further in their careers beyond Alexandra House. To keep cost at a minimal rate, the shelter could take advantage of farmer's markets during the summer seasons to stock up on fresh vegetables such as peppers, onions, tomatoes, and other vegetables that could be improvised to prepare African dishes during the winter when such produce are expensive. In fact, Minnesota is beginning to recognize the impact of having ethnic produce. With many Africans making Minnesota their homes, African grain is being grown in St. Paul. That could be a way to start bringing in and growing African foods in Minnesota for abundance (Hopfensperger). Better still, the Shelter could use some of the space it has in its backyard for gardening. There are various African vegetables that would grow to help reduce the cost of purchases. Also ethnic pot luck could be introduced once every three, or six months, where the women at the shelter will help cooks prepare various dishes from their regions for a special dinner party.

Even though there are alternative solutions, I strongly recommend the introduction of African ethnic food at the Alexandra House. The women will feel a sense of belonging and feel close to home and family traditions (Carol Byrd-Bredbenner). Alexandra House cooks should serve African ethnic food once a week, starting in the fall of 2013 so that African immigrant women who are seeking refuge at the shelter can eat familiar foods to feel more comfortable in their new place of refuge. This will promote cultural exchange among the women and staff of Alexandra House, while the children will learn to embrace other cultures. It will benefit the shelter in the long run. Alexandra House will be operating with the trend of diversity in the state and Anoka County. Most importantly, it will pride itself as a shelter with diversity in all ramifications, including the provisions of tasty foods that cut across various ethnicities.

Works Cited

"African Recipes". SOS Children's Village. SOS Children's Village. SOS-USA, nd. Web. 7 Apr. 2013 K

Alexandra House 2011 Annual Report. Alexandra House., n.d. Web. 16 Apr. 2013. K

Apaloo, Rita. Personal interview. 1 Apr. 2013. INTERVIEW

Balan, Betty. Personal interview. 11 Apr. 2013. INTERVIEW

Carol Byrd-Bredbenner, et al. "Designing Culturally Sensitive Dietary Interventions For African Americans: Review And Recommendations." Nutrition Reviews 71.4 (2013): 224-238. EBSCO MegaFILE. Web. 7 Apr. 2013 L

"Home Grown, Globally Known Popular, versatile, nutritious, convenient, abundant ... Rice!" USA Rice Federation. USA Rice Federation. USA Rice. n.d. Web. 7 Apr. 2013 K

Hopfensperger, Jean. "St. Paul harvests a piece of Africa." Startribune.com. Star Tribune Local, Updated: 5, Sept. 2011. Web. 7 Apr. 2013. C

Lourdes, Medrano L., and Staff Writer. "Immigration: Africans Find they 'have Everything here' ; Minnesota has Become a Migratory Hub for some Groups, Figures show, Including College-Educated Professionals and African Immigrants." Star Tribune Jun 04 2002: 0. ProQuest. PROQUESTMS. 27 Apr. 2013 L

Mamaril, Al. Personal Interview. 30 Apr. 2013 INTERVIEW

Nuokawa, Masataka. Personal Interview. 11 Apr. 2013 INTERVIEW

Peterson, David. "In the Suburbs, Population Growth Sees a Diverse Shift." Star Tribune Aug 07 2008: n/a. ProQuest. PROQUESTMS. 27 Apr. 2013 L

United States Census Bureau. United States Census Bureau., n.d. Web. 16 Apr. 2013 K

Appendix

My Letter to President Obama unedited

August 4, 2016

Attention: President Barack Obama,

CC:Tina Tchen

Assistant to President Barack Obama;

Chief of Staff to First Lady Michelle Obama;

and Executive Director of the White House Council on Women and Girls

The White House

1600 Pennsylvania Avenue NW

Washington, DC 20500

Dear President Barack Obama,

An invitation to meet with you

It's 11:59 PM Central Standard Time in Minnesota. My son is already fast asleep. I couldn't sleep, until I have written this letter to you sir.

I will like to thank you for all your laudable efforts in the United States and around the world. I am particularly grateful for the attention that you have accorded the issue of human trafficking. I write tonight as the secretary to the U.S. Advisory Council on Human Trafficking. The Council that you appointed newly to further enhance the efforts of the federal government in combating human trafficking.

However, I will like to note that this is a great first step. To make this Council deliver to its fullest, to produce the desired result in fighting this heinous crime, the Council needs the continued support, and, especially public support from the office of the President by having the opportunity to meet the president in person. Today, I watched the recorded version of the Live broadcast of the White House on Facebook where you addressed the Young African Leaders Initiative fellows in a town hall meeting with young leaders from across Africa. I think that it will be honorable to have you address the Council in a public forum such as that. It is no longer news that human trafficking affects millions of people around the world, and of that number, are thousands of victims in the United States alone.

The Council has been working tirelessly for the past eight months to produce a report for you and the congress. Sir, I will be grateful if you could be present at a press conference for the Council's report to be announced to the public.

Survivors, who put their faces to their stories like mine dare various consequences to do so. In my own personal experience, I have to think about my safety and that of my nine year old son, even within my Nigerian community. My trafficker died five weeks ago and at first, I felt a sigh of relief. But I couldn't be relieved for too long, because, shortly after, I found myself fearful for my life and the safety of my son. Some people in my community accused me of killing him, because, I put my face to my story, an uncommon thing to do in such a community, for a woman to put her

One of the accusations that I received

face to such a story. But when I think about other people, including men, women, and children who are still suffering under the siege of human trafficking, coupled with domestic violence as it was in my case, I couldn't help myself but to stand up for this people.

For the seven years that I have been on this journey, I have produced a TV show called *Imprisoned Show,* where I have always longed for you to be my dream guest. And, I have made efforts, which have, unfortunately, not been successful to get you on the show.

Now, as a member of the U.S. Advisory Council on Human Trafficking, I will be most grateful if you can host the Advisory Council to a Press conference at the White House in person to launch the release of our first ever report. This will not just send a message of hope to many survivors who have been beaten and battered, and continued to be downgraded even as they strive to play key roles in the community, but will put that seal of safety and approval to this newly formed office. I am very grateful that you took us from nowhere to give us this honorable position, but it will give more credence to have you in person for such an important occasion.

It is commendable that one of us was at the just concluded Democratic National Convention in Pennsylvania, however, having the whole Council and addressing the public in a town hall meeting with the Council will send a message of hope to survivors in sub communities such as mine.

I understand that you are very busy attending to every possible call, but I beg for even 10 to 20 minutes of your time to give us this once in a life time opportunity.

Thank you so much for your time sir.

Respectfully,

Bukola Oriola

Secretary, U.S. Advisory Council on Human Trafficking

I received an email response from Caroline Weber from the White House which read:

Dear Bukola

Thank you for contacting the White House with a scheduling request for President Obama.

President Obama values each and every invitation he receives. However, the constraints of his schedule and the volume of requests are such that the majority of requests must be declined. It is with sincere regret that the President will be unable to accommodate your request.

Thank you for your interest in including the President in your plans. We appreciate your understanding.

Sincerely,
The White House Office of Appointments and Scheduling

Bukola Oriola

Writings from other people unedited

Hello Sister,

It is with great privilege that I write this piece. First and foremost, I will like to thank God for his mercy and love that He had shown upon you and all of us. Just like yesterday, when you were travelling, I was in the university and could remember saying goodbye with joy and happiness, hoping to see you in two weeks or thereabout, little did I know that shortly I will be very afraid and scared for your life. Even though I was afraid, I believed in the faith throughout all the difficult times you went through, they are memories I try not to remember as it brings tears to my eyes.

However, you stood strong, fought for your life and now advocating for others to ensure that people that need help have the required knowledge to be free. What you endure can only be survive by God's grace.

I admire the way you trained Samuel. When I met him, I was really impressed, thank you for been such a good mother. He is so polite, humble, gentle and wise.

Here we are "The Living label" - a living testimony. Thank you for taking such a pain to write this to help others. You are like a mirror and a light for others to see and know that there is hope in every situation.

Lastly, I am so privilege and proud to be your blood brother. God bless you. Love you and Sam.

Abolaji Ogunmola

****

Bukola Oriola, 'Sista' like we usually call her, is my elder and only sister. She is nice to a fault, but a no nonsense person. Decent and a role model like personality, I remember the days we would have vigils in the house that my sister insisted we do. Morning devotion was compulsory, thanks to her, even though, most mornings, I was not always in the mood, because devotion time was 6:00 a.m., I think. But the prayers worked immensely. She was my sleeping partner too, and I loved to wear her dresses whenever she had gone to work. As young as I was, I always wanted to look chic and she had a lovely taste, very hardworking, and generous. She reminded me of our late mum. Asides from the physical resemblance, she had our mum's behavioral characteristics.

The last time that I saw her was at the airport in 2005 until September, 2015 when she came to Nigeria for Bringing the Story Back Home, a campaign and awareness on the human trafficking issue, her story and tips to battling the issue and the fact that there is help available for victims.

Going for the U.N. conference in the United States in 2005 to me felt like a huge stepping stone in her career, but all that was cut short when she entered into that marriage with her husband, who became her trafficker. My sister is a lovely person with a sweet personality. She is a very strong lady. To pull through all she had gone through, I would say that I duff my hat for her.

I thank God for his kindness over her and her son. She has suffered a lot but I thank God for the greater plans He has for her and Sam. We have our differences, but she is a good sister.

September 2015 was the first and only time that I have seen Sam, and as I write this part of A Living Label book. We got along so well. I also enjoyed swimming with him during his short visit to Nigeria. Sam is a lot older in thoughts than his age. He is a son sent from God to Bukola. He is so understanding and adorable, I love him. I am grateful for the privilege given to me to write in ALL book. I pray it touches the heart of everybody that reads it, and that it helps survivors as well. I love you, Bukola Oriola

Anuoluwapo Ogunmola
Owner, House of Fancy

****

How does one survive a new universe? Culture? Language? Separation from family?

Add full-time mother (single parent), business woman, fundraiser, public access television show producer, author, student, human trafficking survivor and advocate to the mix and a single word comes to mind – that word is Bukola.

The Yoruban name means blessing upon honor. Aptly named, Bukola Oriola humbly encapsulates both – the blessings she brings to other trafficking victims and the honor of service she bestows upon them.

I first spoke with Bukola at great length in 2010 at our newspaper office in Coon Rapids, Minn. I had read her book, "Imprisoned: The Travails of a Trafficked Victim," and wanted to follow up with a feature story. She appeared for the interview with her then three-year-old son, Sammy, in tow.

Because Bukola had relocated from Nigeria, initially, we muddled through a few language barrier issues. But upon my request, she graciously wrote the words in question on a piece of paper. We later laughed about our efforts to communicate. She knew that I was striving for accuracy because she had been a reporter in her homeland.

I later visited Bukola in her braiding shop. Her story unraveled as she braided customers' hair.

Amid all of her trafficking hardships - isolation, verbal and sexual abuse, hunger and long working hours only to have her pay taken away, to name a few - she managed to maintain her sense of dignity. She overcame heinous obstacles. Ultimately, she emerged a victor.

Bukola has been on a mission for some time now. She wants people suffering similar traumas to know that help is available "instead of becoming a statistic," she said in the story I penned about her in the Anoka County Union. (For a computer search, see "Victim of human trafficking turns life around," Feb. 25, 2010.)

Bukola is a survivor. She is resilient and tenacious. When she was able, she turned her altruistic deeds outward to help other abuse and human trafficking victims.

She welcomed guests to a Minnesota regional park where she spearheaded a free barbeque fund-raiser. She donated the proceeds and school supplies to families at a women's shelter. She didn't want any child to go without. She wanted to help children as Sammy had been helped when they stayed at the shelter.

But her untiring dedication didn't stop there. She continues to speak at innumerable functions on the atrocities of human trafficking. She works to help victims find solutions. Communicating is among her many strong points as she moves forward with her calling to deliver her anti-trafficking message nationwide. She has brought her message to Nigeria as well.

And I would be remiss not to mention Bukola's unwavering sense of humor and infectious smile. Despite her past, she radiates a certain ebullient zeal for life. In short, she is a joy.

In 2016 she was appointed to serve on the U.S. Advisory Council on Human Trafficking.

"Now, I am stepping out to speak, to take the shame for everybody," Bukola said about human trafficking in the 2010 Anoka County Union article. "So that victims who need help can hold onto my shame as a ladder and climb it to get help that is available."

Steadfast. Infinite crusader. Educator. Problem solver. Glowing spirit. Blessing upon honor. Love. That is Bukola.

Elyse Kaner is a retired reporter and arts editor for ABC Newspapers in Minnesota.

****

I wasn't tuned in to human trafficking until I became aware of Bukola's story. Before then, my human trafficking knowledge was limited to sex trafficking. Basically, I thought it only happened to certain kind of people of whom I did not know and had no connections. As far as I was concerned, human trafficking was a taboo subject in my community—the African immigrant community. Therefore I did not pay much attention to it and hoped and prayed that it would never happen to anyone I knew.

What I was positively aware of and passionate about was the need to provide opportunities for African women to connect and expand their network for friendship, business and community. I did this through African Women Connect, an organization I founded in 2004, with the purpose of creating a space for African women to share information, learn from and support each other, and have fun socializing while building meaningful relationships. It was through this medium that I came to know Bukola Oriola. I had met a friend of a friend through African Women Connect and was invited to an event that Bukola was also attending. She was fun and charming and I became interested in her journalism background and her work with a local newspaper as a contributing writer. I was hoping that she would write a story about AWC to spread the word about the organization to a larger audience of women. She did just that and AWC did get a lot of interest from that article. However, soon after that, she disappeared and I could no longer contact her through the information she shared with me. This was not completely uncommon in the African community— people often voluntarily isolated themselves, believing they are better off with less drama from being surrounded by fellow Africans-- however they defined that to be-- so I didn't give it much thought.

I later learned that Bukola and her husband had moved way out to the suburbs, in an area not generally populated by immigrants or people of color. I was taken aback and, interestingly, I wondered if the move had anything to do with any intentions to isolate her from the little support system she had but I ignored my gut feeling and convinced myself that I was being overly paranoid. I would find much later that my gut feeling was indeed spot-on.

Fast forward a couple of months later, one early Sunday morning while making a quick run to the store for milk and eggs for breakfast, I received a call from Bukola, who was clearly upset and in distress. In that moment, I honestly felt that I was prepared to help her because of my participation in AWC all those years and months, learning to build meaningful relationships and support other women. I was grateful for the trust she placed in my ability to assist her and I immediately launched into action. With my help, along with many others along the way, Bukola survived and is now helping victims and empowering survivors or human trafficking and abuse.

Since then, I have become more aware of human trafficking, as well as many others who have heard her story. Today I know that there several types of human trafficking including sex, labor and organ. Research shows that building relationships outside of one's close-knit circle can be life-saving. This is something I had been sharing through AWC prior to learning about Bukola's story and I continue to share even more today. Bukola's memoir

Imprisoned: The Travails of a Human trafficked Victim, demonstrates how easily a person could find themselves stuck in a small circle of influence, where group-think is the song and dance and even when the person is crying for help, those in the circle either don't hear it, dismisses it or misinterprets it for something else. They often can't see beyond the small circle. When we breakaway we often have a chance to have a different and more liberating experience, like Bukola did.

Bukola's story is a gift to all, especially to African women and girls because they can easily relate to her experiences and understand the context. Bukola is brave, bold and determined in her work on human trafficking and domestic abuse and the cultural perspective that her story adds to the conversation is so very important in addressing issues around abuse in all communities. I don't take this gift lightly. In fact, I intentionally use Bukola's story in my work as a community educator and leader. Her story and wisdom provide us with a powerful tool to educate and empower women, girls and all people to breakout of patterns and relationships that keep them captive when they can be free, empowered and happy.

I am inspired by her courage to not only move forward but also to create the kind of life she wants and deserves, no matter what the challenges are or the naysayers claim. Above all, her faith is steadfast and her confidence and dignity are intact. I am honored to work with her, learn from her and celebrate with her any chance I get.

In gratitude,

Rita Apaloo

******

Dear Bukola Oriola,

I want to express to you, the joy that I feel deep in my soul for having the honor of meeting you. I admire you for your strength, dedication, sacrifices, honesty, passion, compassion and all the love you put in everything you do. I try to find the right word to describe you, but I still can't find the perfect one that might define who you really are.

Since the first moment I met you during a Survivor Forum in Washington in 2014, I adore you. I could witness how passionate you were advocating for the survivors' rights. I listened to your story and it amazed me just by seeing the way you overcome your trafficking situation. I applaud you for standing up.

I really enjoy being around you. You make me laugh, you are very enthusiastic and always with a positive attitude toward any circumstance. You are yourself no matter who is around. You don't change because of the circumstances. Please always be you and never ever change.

But the most I love about you is that even though you have lots of talents given to you by the Lord, you are still humble and very helpful with anyone who needs your help. You are what I call a true friend. Thank you Bukola for all your support, I deeply appreciate everything you have done for me and for a lot of survivors.

I wish you all the best in your new book "A Living Label" and in your future. Thank you for taking your time to write this book and for designing the money resulting of the sales to help survivors in need.

God bless you and your family.

Best regards,

Ronny Marty, Member, U.S. Advisory Council on Human Trafficking

******

Bukola Oriola has changed my perspective on the world. I don't say that lightly. As a feminist theologian, I was aware of the prevalence and tragic effects of human trafficking. However, it is one thing to know *about* an issue and quite another to know a *person* who has experienced it in their own life.

I first came to know Bukola as a member of my church, the United Methodist Church of Anoka. Her reputation had preceded her; church members and my husband (the pastor) told me about this extraordinary and dynamic woman. I soon learned that her reputation was well deserved and I joined the board of the non-profit she founded, the Enitan Story. My years serving on this board and knowing Bukola has helped me to learn some important truths:

Anyone can become a victim of human trafficking. Bukola was a journalist in Nigeria and a woman of incredible strength and intelligence. If she can become a victim of human trafficking, anyone can. The situation, not the characteristics of the individual, is the primary factor in this crime.

"Victim of human trafficking" describes a person who has experienced a terrible crime and an abuse of human dignity. It is not their only, or even primary, identity. Bukola, for example, is a business owner, an activist, a writer, a student, a church member, a mother, and a friend. It is a further affront to the dignity of those who have suffered human trafficking to make that their primary identity.

Victims of human trafficking can be subject to re-exploitation, even by non-profit organizations that claim to be helping them. Bukola's story has been used – without her permission – by organizations seeking to raise money. This is part of a larger problem of individuals or organizations using victims of human trafficking for their own purposes.

In all these, and many other ways, Bukola has changed my perspective on the world. More importantly, Bukola is working to change the world, to make it a more just and compassionate place for everyone. She does so with amazing energy and creativity. Her efforts range from hosting a local television show, planting a community garden to grow ethnic foods, traveling to Nigeria to speak to college students, responding to the needs of individuals who contact her via social media, and writing books. Her recent appointment to serve as a member of the U.S. Advisory Council on Human Trafficking is a testament to her past achievements and a position that will enable her to accomplish even more in the future. I look forward to seeing what that extraordinary woman will do in the years ahead as she continues to live out the mission of the Enitan Story: "to advocate for victims and empower survivors of human trafficking and domestic violence".

Dr. Sherry Jordon, Associate Professor, University of St. Thomas, St. Paul, MN

****

It was August 2010 when Bukola – and as I now fondly call her Buky - entered my life. She was seeking marketing help for her hair braiding company. Seemed

innocuous enough. Help this young lady with the strange accent to do some basic marketing, and watch as her business prosper. Her eyes looked at me with uncertainty and anxious hope as she told about her business. I said something that must have been amusing when a big smile with that trademark gap in her teeth shown brightly and her infectious laugh burst forth. That laugh. It has come to comfort me and lift me up many times over the years. I knew then and there that I met a very special person. Bukola Love Oriola. Here was a woman from the other side of the world who was about as far from a small town Minnesota Scandanavian like me as one could be. We were miles apart in culture, age, race, and background yet I felt somehow deeply connected. Buky and I became friends quickly and soon arranged a time to go to the

146

Minnesota State Fair with her son Sam. We met at the agreed place and time and as I peered into the backseat of her car, I saw the little man that would forever change my life. Sam's head was drooping and he had a scowl on his face because he was disappointed he had to leave his friends in order to come to the fair with us. The look was almost comical. Tentative at first, Sam warmed up to me as the three of us walked the fair. I bought him a little bubble making gun and a huge grin beamed across his face. It was that moment I fell in love with the little guy. I found Sam and Sam found me. We needed each other and our lives would never be the same.

I come from a big family. Six sisters, one brother, and 35 nieces and nephews. I absolutely LOVE kids and am known as the proverbial "Uncle Joe" to many. I look at this little boy Sam and reflect on the irony that out of the ugliness of human trafficking could emerge a soul that one could not help but love. Sam is an old soul. He is wise beyond his years. The joy he spreads is an extension of Buyk's heart and I consider myself lucky to be part of their life. God must have been smiling from heaven the day Sam came into this world. My own family quickly welcomed them into our hearts and homes. They fit right in to our family events and vacations despite a huge cultural gap. There have been adjustments in our relationship over the years but despite all the differences love still binds us together. They will always be family to me.

Trafficking is a terrible, terrible, thing. It destroys people's lives, their souls, and the people around it suffer as well. It is evil through and through and it can be happening right in front of us, hidden in plain sight. Over the years, I have traveled with Buky to human trafficking speeches she gave, fundraising events, and conferences. It never ceased to amaze me how Buky touched hearts wherever we went. I watched as people came out of their imprisoned lives to claim that they too were victims. I began to wonder where the line was between "normal" life and a trafficked life. To the casual observer, a couple with a tumultuous relationship may be viewed just as a bad relationship but through my life with Buky and Sam I have learned to look deeper. I learned that right here in our hometowns in the USA people are held against their will by force, by financial pressures, and by threats. Some are forced to work by their captor and some are forced to do unconciable things such as rape, drugs, and theft. Yet many people in the world that see their painful, imprisoned existence as normal forge ahead and endure the suffering inflicted on them by the traffickers.

Millions of people who are held captive now are suffering. Buky has certainly suffered as a result of trafficking and I know her son Sam suffers too. They both carry a burden financially, emotionally, and psychologically. To most, the experience they have lived would drain the spirit from their hearts and the smile from their face. So where does Buky's trademark smile and infectious laugh get it's life from? It comes from all of us as we reach out to victims and help them through their struggles. We have all heard the saying "God works in mysterious ways" and I have come to feel that about Sam and Buky. They have both brought so much joy and happiness into my life and the lives of others. I truly believe they are a conduit for God to spread joy and healing throughout the world. God Bless them both.

Joe Hesch – "Uncle Joe"

****

Human trafficking is a travesty that moves people, but it is not contained in a bubble. Bukola is someone who has been a large influence and continues to broaden my perception of the realities of human trafficking. As an advocate who has never personally experienced trafficking, I must be conscious that there is always more to learn. The key is to actively listen. Listening is the only true way to understand the realities of someone's experience, and the trials and tribulations that follow a survivor afterward.

Bukola Oriola and I met as students at Metropolitan State University. Through the time we have known each other she has been a constant beam of light and energy, whether it is at The Enitan Story office or a brief coffee shop meeting. Her dedication and commitment to empowering survivors of human trafficking and domestic violence is unwavering. When Bukola approached

149

me about embarking with her on a new project I jumped right on top of the idea. Students Against Abuse and Slavery International (SAASI) was the child of Bringing the Story Back Home, a human trafficking awareness tour visiting Nigerian universities. Due to the students' excitement, Bukola saw an opportunity to bring human trafficking awareness to students and their communities on a global level.

After beginning the complex journey of SAASI, we decided to launch a social media contest. Students were encouraged to post a picture, video, etc. on the SAASI Facebook page to share tools within their community that would spread human trafficking awareness. One entry was immediately noticed by Bukola, a picture with tied up hands. This did not strike me as damaging until Bukola explained the dramatization further. While I saw the picture as an artistic representation, it was not apparent to me that it was perpetuating false myths about human trafficking and the public understanding of victims' and survivors' experiences. While I saw an artistic expression, in the eyes of a survivor it was a false representation, disregarding the majority of victims hidden in plain sight, most often not forced or coerced through physical restraint. Through this lesson, Bukola alerted me to the significance a single image can have. I became attuned to the effects that reverberate through media and incorrect narratives surrounding human trafficking.

This was one of many lessons Bukola has taught me, and I'm sure there will be many more. A Living Label is an opportunity to understand the complex nature of Bukola's journey, and I look forward to continuing to learn every lesson I can through these pages. Bukola, you have touched so many lives through your empowerment and work. I know that this book will impact countless others. Your friendship is priceless and I look forward to the future change that stems from this publication. Your words and actions will continue to prevent human trafficking and educate communities internationally for decades to come.

Sarah Leistico

Social Justice Organizer & SAASI U.S. Coordinator

Based in Minneapolis- St. Paul, MN

****

Service-Learning Case Study

Dr. Abimbola O. Asojo, University of Minnesota

Current trends in higher education are promoting service-learning a teaching methodology that incorporates community service opportunities into academic curriculum as a way of improving students learning outcomes and promoting civic engagement. This article discusses pedagogical experiences and

151

lessons learned from a service-learning project accomplished in sophomore interior design courses in spring 2013 at the University of Minnesota. Students gained disciplinary and civic benefits while design problem solving for the mobile TV set for the Imprisoned Show dedicated to advocating for victims of human trafficking on Minnesota public television with show producer, Bukola Oriola.

The goal of this project was to expose interior design students to issues of human trafficking through design problem solving for the set of the Imprisoned Show on a Minnesota public television channel. The Imprisoned show is dedicated to preventing human trafficking in the community through public awareness and enlightening the community using broadcast media. The program also advocates for victims and reaches out to survivors. The class collaborated with Bukola Oriola (show producer), the camera team, the editor, and the television station personnel. The set had to be mobile, easily assembled and disassembled with ease. The budget for the actual set was $1,000 for the furniture which did not include the lighting or any production equipment. Funding was secured by the author from the 2012-2013 Fairchild Topical issue grant sponsored by Fairchild books to implement the design. Since the show is multicultural, the lighting design had to be appropriate for all skin tones.

The project occurred over a two-week period with class meeting two days a week in spring semester 2013. On day one students toured the studios in North Metro TV station in Blaine,

Minnesota and interviewed the client. On day two, students developed conceptual and schematic ideas. On day three, students developed their final presentations. On day four, students presented their design solutions to the client. Twenty-five students split into eight groups presented their design proposals to the client (Figure 1). The design solution selected by the client used warm tones complimented with blue and white tones of the Imprisoned show. Three director's chairs, a side table, a custom rug with Imprisoned show logo and a banner were used to create the final mobile set (Figure 2).

Figure 1: Design proposals by the students

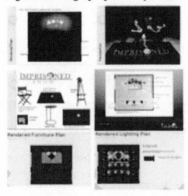

Figure2: Actual Set

Design problem solving for the Imprisoned show TV set offered students many disciplinary and civic benefits such as relevance to course objectives, application of course knowledge, connection to community, and an opportunity to reflect on their

153

learning. In terms of application of course knowledge, students were able to apply their course knowledge of the lighting design process to problem-solving for the TV set. Students met with client and toured the television station, next they researched and developed conceptual ideas for the set, next they presented their schematic designs to the client and finally, they presented their presentation drawings to the client. In terms of connection to the community, students were able to connect with the producer of the TV show, TV studio manager and other support staff to determine requirements for the space. Student reflections occurred in debriefing sessions throughout the project and at the end of the project.

The class overwhelming welcomed and supported the idea of design problem solving for real life clients and how this community engagement service-learning projects increased their knowledge of issues impacting the community. The service-learning project also increased students' sensitivity to and empathy for community challenges and issues related to human trafficking. It also offered students an opportunity to bridge the gap between theory and practice through design experiences in real life authentic settings. Students also developed their communication and collaboration skills through connection with a variety of professionals on a real life project.

A Living Label

Abimbola Asojo, Ph.D., is a Professor of Interior Design in the Department of Design, Housing and Apparel at the College of Design, University of Minnesota. Her research focuses on cross-cultural design issues, African architecture, computing and design, lighting design, and global design. Her research has been disseminated in the Journal of Interior Design, International Journal of Architectural Research, Traditional Dwellings and Settlements Review, and the Handbook of Interior Design. She is a licensed architect in the state of Oklahoma and holds a National Council for Interior Design Qualification (NCIDQ) certification. She is a member of the Interior Design Educators Council (IDEC), the American Institute of Architects (AIA) and the Illuminating Engineering Society (IES). She is a LEED Accredited Professional and also serves on the Journal of Interior Design (JID) Review board and the Illuminating Engineering Society (IES. In 2010, Asojo was honored as one of the top 25 most admired educators in the United States by Design Intelligence.

****

Until I met Bukola Oriola sometime in 2003, I was a timid, naive and fearful young lady haven suffered many years of low self esteem.

Bold, daring, down to earth, resilient, committed, loving and full of life, Bukky, as I fondly call her drew me close and pumped possibilities into me, making me realize that with absolute trust in God and unwavering determination to succeed, all things are possible.

155

We were soon to become not just close friends but sisters who loved, cared and confided in each other without looking down or denigrating each other.

My greatest critic and cheerleader, Bukky never hesitated to tell me how bad or how good I had been while also showing me other ways of doing things better.

An award winning journalist who had traveled a few other countries before sojourning to the United States of America (USA), no one could imagine such a beautiful soul would pass through what Bukky went through in a far away country with no relation or friend close by.

But being who she is, Bukky lived up to expectation and came out of her predicament stronger, more determined and more emboldened to look failure in the face yet tow the path of success in life.

I am not surprised that she could turn her story around from an imprisoned soul to a living label after climbing so many ladders to be where she is today.

A mother, student, educator, activist, writer and a workaholic to the core, Bukky can go many extra miles to meet the needs of others and make them happy.

As you launch yet another book, I can only pray that you continue to find joy in what you do and radiate same to as many as will come in contact with you.

Rose EJEMBI is a Senior Correspondent with The Sun Newspapers (Nigeria).

******

It is said that to fully understand what another person is experiencing, one needs to actually "walk in his footsteps." The reality of pain, fear, uncertainty, and hopelessness then becomes more clear.

Bukola Oriola, my friend, adopted "granddaughter" and Sister in Christ, is a survivor of human trafficking. This situation completely changed her life and its direction. She WAS a victim but IS now an advocate. She suffered abuse but has also been the recipient of police protection, safe housing, counseling, legal and medical services, and lots of T.L.C. from community and church organizations. In fact Bukola founded her own non-profit organization called "The Enitan Story" to provide similar resources and financing for victims and survivors of trafficking and domestic violence.

As a very committed advocate, Bukola adamantly uses her journalist skills and tech skills to create educational material for publications, for T. V. and websites, for civic groups, and for school textbooks. She has also authored two autobiographical books – *Imprisoned: The Travails of a Trafficked Victim* and *A Living*

Label.

As a captivating public speaker, she is in great demand.
Bukola tells her moving story very well and educates her
audiences about human trafficking issues as well: What is human
trafficking and who are its victims? How can a victim be
identified? What can be done to develop a victim's trust?. What
are the differences in sex, labor, and organ trafficking?
Educating the public is a huge part of Bukola's work.

At present, Bukola serves on the President's Advisory
Council for Human Trafficking in Washington, D. C. advising the
government. Her impact became international with her 2016
"Bringing The Story Home" trip to Nigeria. Much interaction
with Nigerian government officials and the media brought the
topic of Human Trafficking to the forefront of the news.
Support for this trip abroad was given her by Metro State
University of MN, Bukola's alma mater. This ten day trip
provided many learning opportunities for both sponsors. College
presentations inspired captivated audiences of young people who
wanted to make contributions to this cause. Future cooperative
events have been proposed for next year's studies.

I feel blessed to have Bukola Oriola as a caring friend!! She
is strong in spirit, very gifted, compassionate, devoted to her
cause and full of zeal to share challenges with others! She
exemplifies how to "love your neighbor." Her faith, hard work
and dedication have positively influenced so many lives. As a

healed victim, she now serves those in bondage who are on a journey to wholeness and health.

Annette Brandner

****

Dear Bukola,

I first became acquainted with you through a friend who was a client at your braiding salon. My friend mentioned she was getting her hair braided and had been reading a story about a woman in the African News Journal who was a trafficking survivor. Little did I know that survivor was you. I became intrigued about the hair braiding and the story. I eventually became a client and on one of our hair braiding appointments I purchased the book from you about your story. I was moved to tears. I wept bitterly at what you went through and also wept because you survived. Not only did you survive but you exudes optimism and tell your story with great conviction and enthusiasm to audiences globally.

One thing that impressed me the most was that you pray before starting on my hair. I knew then that I had found a kindred soul to trust with my hair and my life issues. A hairstylist is more than just a stylist, you become family and a safe place to share the issues of life. I watched you gracefully care for your son in the shop; feeding him and speaking to him in Yoruba language. I admired your child rearing because it so much reminded me of how I reared my sons.

I was so moved by your courage and tenacity that I wanted to become a part of whatever you were doing for the cause of trafficking. Hence I received an invitation to become a board member of The Enitan Story. I have been part of member meetings and events such as the women's sewing class, empowerment sessions, graduation of clients and social media awareness.

You are an inspiration to women and anyone who desires to bounce back from a trial in their life. You are indeed a living label, a true testament of what faith can do. I have come to call you friend but you are more like a sister who cares for me when I need encouragement. You offer that through laughter, stories, food, checking on me and more. I do not know how you manage all that you do because truly your plate is full and your cup runneth over. But I do know by God's grace, mercy and favor you do it effortlessly.

Additionally, I want to say your business acumen is bar none. You simplify business concepts and ideas where the average person can comprehend and do it without hesitation or fear. You are a joyful woman with a sense of humor and lightens and livens any place you happen to be. I pray you the best in your future endeavors and as we say 'more grease to your elbow'.

Warm regards,

Yvette R. Toko

Owner, Healing Words with Yvette

****

My name is Isabella Kerubo Ongera, I am a Kenyan-American woman who is very passionate about women empowerment. I have known Bukola Oriola for slightly over ten years now. While I was living in Minnesota, USA, Bukola was my hair dresser. For the first one year that I went to her house in Anoka to have my hair done, I had no clue that behind that smile I could see on Bukola's face there was torture and sorrow. We could talk and laugh and share stories about our countries back in Africa and so on while her then little son Sam was playing with his toys on the floor. Occasionally little Sam could demand for his mother's attention and Bukola could take a break, feed him and wrap him on her back to sleep just the way we rock babies to sleep back in Africa.

One evening, I called Bukola to place my hair appointment for the next morning 6:00 a.m. She requested me to pick her up from a "friend's house," whom she had gone to visit in Blaine. She gave me directions up to a gas station on University Avenue in Blaine which was near the "friend's house." She then gave me her "friend's" phone number to call her once I arrived since she didn't have her phone with her.

Next morning at 6:00 a.m., I was at the gas station, temperatures were below zero and there came Bukola with little Sam wrapped on her back. Every time I talk about Bukola's story to the women I meet, this picture of Bukola with her baby on her back walking in snow in a terribly cold morning passes through my mind.

By this time Bukola had opened a small hair salon in Anoka. When we arrived at the salon, this was the day Bukola opened up to me about the hell of life she was living in her husband's house. It turned out that the "friend's house" where I picked her from was actually a shelter for battered women where she had been seeking refuge. I remember us crying on each other's shoulders that morning, it felt like I was listening to a horror story.

Bukola's story made me think and look at life from different angles. It made me realize that a lot of women are going through so many forms of abuse silently without reporting because they fear for so many things that have been instilled in their minds by the perpetrators. The abuse compromise their self-esteem up to

162

an extent that the victims are unable to stand up for themselves and say NO to what is not right.

I thought about all sorts of abuse that women go through in my community back in my country Kenya. That is how I started thinking of registering an NGO back in Kenya that would run empowerment programs for women and girls. I registered the organization in 2014 and among the programs we run is celebrating and empowering survivors of Female Genital Mutilation (FGM), a very cruel form of violence against women which is practiced in my community. FGM is one of the leading causes of Fistula among women in my community. FGM lowers women's libido thus a lot of women have been abandoned by their husbands who opt to marry women who haven't gone through FGM. Through this program, the women survivors are getting to know that all is not lost. The program is helping them to realize that they can pick up their broken pieces and rebuild their lives all over again.

My bigger dream is to help all the FGM survivors who have suffered with the stigma reawaken their lost self-esteem and economically empower them to be economically independent and bring up healthy families since most of them live below poverty. I will forever dedicate this program to Ms. Bukola Oriola who has always been my inspiration.

Isabella Kerubo Ongera

Vinbel Foundation

Acronyms

ACCAP: Anoka County Community Action Program

AWC: African Women Connect

SAASI: Students Against Abuse and Slavery International

BTSBH: Bringing The Story Back Home

FAIM: Family Assets for Independence in Minnesota

IRS: Internal revenue Service

LLC: Limited Liability Company

OVC: Office for Victims of Crime

OVCTTAC: Office for Victims of Crime Training and Technical Assistance Center

PITF: President's Interagency Task Force to Combat Trafficking in Persons

PTSD: Post Traumatic Stress Disorder

SESP: Survivor Empowerment Sewing Program

SOS: Secretary of State

TVPA: Trafficking Victim Protection Act 2000

NAPTIP: National Agency for the Prohibition of Trafficking in Persons

United States Agency for International Development

VAWA: Violence Against Women Act

Made in the USA
Monee, IL
27 October 2020

46212601R00104